Modern Life Skills for Young Adults 2.0

The Essential Handbook to Make Money, Beat Procrastination, Build Strong Relationships, and Enjoy Independence Without Overwhelm

---

Daily Balance Journals

© **Copyright 2025 - All rights reserved.**

The content within this book may not be reproduced, duplicated or transmitted without direct written permission from the author or the publisher.

Under no circumstances will any blame or legal responsibility be held against the publisher, or author, for any damages, reparation, or monetary loss due to the information contained within this book. Either directly or indirectly. You are responsible for your own choices, actions, and results.

Legal Notice:

This book is copyright protected. This book is only for personal use. You cannot amend, distribute, sell, use, quote or paraphrase any part of the content within this book, without the consent of the author or publisher.

Disclaimer Notice:

This book is intended for informational and educational purposes only. The advice and strategies contained herein may not be suitable for every situation. This work is sold with the understanding that the author and publisher are not engaged in rendering legal, accounting, or other professional services. If professional assistance is required, the services of a competent professional should be sought.

Neither the publisher nor the author shall be liable for damages arising therefrom. The fact that an individual, organization, or website is referred to in this work as a citation and/or a potential source of further information does not mean that the author or the publisher endorses the information the individual, organization, or website may provide or recommendations they may make.

Furthermore, readers should be aware that Internet websites listed in this work may have changed or disappeared between when this work was written and when it was read. No warranty may be created or extended by any promotional statements for this work.

Financial Disclaimer:

This book contains financial information and advice specific to the United States. The financial strategies and examples provided herein are only for informational purposes and may not apply in other jurisdictions. The author and publisher are not financial advisors; this book does not provide personalized financial, legal, or tax advice. Readers are encouraged to consult professional advisors for advice tailored to their circumstances. The author and publisher disclaim any liability, loss, or risk taken by individuals who directly or indirectly act on the information provided in this book. All readers are advised to perform their due diligence when making financial decisions.

Table of Contents

Bonus!!!	9
Preface	11
Introduction	13
1. BEATING PROCRASTINATION	17
1.1 Understanding the Root Causes of Procrastination	18
1.2 Practical Strategies to Combat Procrastination	20
1.3 Digital Tools to Boost Your Productivity	22
1.4 Designing a Personal Productivity System	24
1.5 Embracing Progress Over Perfection	27
1.6 Transform with Cognitive Restructuring	29
2. MASTERING TIME MANAGEMENT	33
2.1 Prioritize Tasks With the Eisenhower Box	33
2.2 Time Blocking: A Guide to Maximizing Your Day	37
2.3 Digital Detox: Reclaiming Your Time From Screens	38
2.4 Setting Boundaries to Protect Your Time	40
2.5 The Art of Saying No: Protect Your Priorities	42
3. DECISION-MAKING AND PROBLEM-SOLVING SKILLS	45
3.1 Decision-Making Frameworks for Important Life Choices	46
3.2 Problem-Solving Techniques for Everyday Challenges	49
3.3 Overcoming Indecisiveness: Gaining Confidence in Your Choices	51
3.4 The Role of Intuition in Decision-Making	53
3.5 Learning From Mistakes: Turning Failures Into Opportunities	54

4. HEALTH AND WELLNESS IN A FAST-PACED
   WORLD   57
   4.1 Establishing a Daily Self-Care Routine   58
   4.2 Nutrition on a Budget   60
   4.3 Incorporating Exercise into Daily Life   61
   4.4 Understanding Sleep and Recovery   63
   4.5 Stress Management Techniques   64
   4.6 Mindfulness Practices   66

5. ENHANCING EMOTIONAL AND MENTAL WELL-
   BEING   69
   5.1 Mindfulness and Meditation Techniques   70
   5.2 Developing Resilience and Coping Skills   72
   5.3 Self-Care for Mental Health   75
   5.4 Recognizing When to Seek Help   77

6. BUILDING AND MAINTAINING RELATIONSHIPS   79
   6.1 Communication Techniques for Stronger
   Connections   80
   6.2 Conflict Resolution Strategies for Peaceful
   Outcomes   81
   6.3 Maintaining Healthy Boundaries with Friends
   and Family   83
   6.4 Roommate Dynamics   86
   6.5 Romantic Relationships in the Digital Age   88
   6.6 Building a Supportive Social Network   90

7. NAVIGATING COLLEGE LIFE   95
   7.1 Choosing the Right Housing   96
   7.2 Effective Study Techniques   98
   7.3 Balancing Work and Study   100
   7.4 Engaging Campus Life   102

8. CRAFTING YOUR CAREER PATH   105
   8.1 Building Professional Networks from Scratch   105
   8.2 Crafting a Standout Resume and Cover Letter   107
   8.3 Mastering the Art of the Job Interview   110
   8.4 Navigating Workplace Culture: Tips for Success   112
   8.5 Leveraging Digital Platforms for Career Growth   114

9. MONEY MATTERS   117
   9.1 Understanding Money Basics   118
   9.2 Create a Budget That Works for You   119

9.3 Saving for Emergencies and Future Goals	121
9.4 Understanding Credit Scores and How to Improve Yours	121
9.5 The Basics of Tax and Tax Filing	122
9.6 Tackling Student Loans Strategically	124
9.7 Managing Debt Wisely	125
9.8 Earning and Negotiating	127
9.9 Investing 101: Building Wealth for the Long Term	128
9.10 Avoiding Common Financial Pitfalls	130
10. CULTIVATING AN ENTREPRENEURIAL MINDSET	**133**
10.1 Identifying Opportunities: Seeing Problems as Possibilities	133
10.2 The Basics of Starting Your Own Business	135
10.3 Intrapreneurship: Career Innovation	137
10.4 Building Resilience in the Face of Failure	139
10.5 Networking With an Entrepreneurial Mindset	141
11. EMBRACING MODERN CHALLENGES	**145**
11.1 Navigating Remote Work: Tips to Stay Productive	146
11.2 Building a Personal Brand in the Digital Age	148
11.3 Digital Etiquette: Managing Your Online Presence	150
11.4 Understanding and Embracing Diversity and Inclusion	152
12. THE PURSUIT OF CONTINUOUS GROWTH AND LEARNING	**155**
12.1 The Importance of Lifelong Learning	156
12.2 Interactive Element: Personal Learning Plan	157
12.3 Developing Critical Thinking Skills	158
12.4 Find Inspiration in Books Instead of Quick Online Fixes	161
Conclusion	165
References	169

Bonus!!!

A Special Gift for You! As a heartfelt thank you from the bottom of my heart, dive into this exclusive guide designed to help you see obstacles as chances for growth and success.

Scan the QR code below:

"Reframing 50 Real-Life Challenges into 50 Opportunities"

"The future belongs to those who learn more skills and combine them in creative ways."

Robert Greene

Introduction

On a typical weekday as a student, you might be buried under a mountain of scholastic assignments, juggling a part-time job and trying to maintain a happy social life. But deadline pressures feel heavy at times, and your phone notifications never seem to stop. It's easy to feel overwhelmed by a cascade of responsibilities and expectations. So, ***please pause and take a deep breath;*** you're not alone. This is a reality today for many young adults.

This book aims to help you navigate those challenges by equipping you with practical skills to ***handle modern life's challenges, reduce overwhelm, and enhance your independence***. Here, you'll find a toolkit of strategies that empower you to take control of your life (at least when it comes to school).

I envision this book as a supportive companion packed with ***actionable advice, reflective questions, and exercises***. It's meant to inspire you to think beyond present challenges and cultivate an entrepreneurial mindset to encourage you to view life as a series of opportunities to grow, learn, and create.

Let's *reflect and connect* at this point in your life. You're transitioning to adulthood, a time filled with its unique set of struggles and ambitions, particularly for those of you in early or mid-career. You naturally want to succeed in your studies, build a career, make money, and form meaningful relationships that foster a well-balanced life. This book is tailored to help you do just that by acknowledging your experiences, goals, and a framework to navigate your future with confidence.

Developing life skills and soft skills is crucial in today's busy world. While the internet offers endless streams of information, much of it can be fleeting and superficial. This book focuses on providing effective tools and substantial knowledge that help you build a *strong foundation* for a sound future.

Within these pages, you will learn key topics such as *overcoming procrastination, being financially savvy, building strong relationships, and maintaining a healthy work-life balance.* Each chapter features insights and practical steps to help you develop and apply those skills to your daily life.

I'm passionate about guiding young adults to *take action, gain more confidence,* and *just enjoy their lives*! YOLO! I've seen how these skills can transform lives, and I'm committed to sharing this knowledge with you. I aim to support you in creating a life that best reflects your values and aspirations.

By the end of this book, you will have the knowledge and tools to steer your life in the direction you choose. You'll learn to see your journey as a *growth process* rather than a destination. Yes, you will make mistakes like everyone else, but you'll see them as transformational opportunities to learn and improve.

To make the most of this book, use it to suit your needs. It's structured for flexibility, so you can jump to any relevant section that interests you. Concentrate on topics that resonate with your most substantial needs and interests. I encourage you to actively engage the lessons herein by practicing the exercises and reflecting on personal experience to help internalize its lessons and apply them to your life.

So, you are about to embark on a journey of self-improvement and empowerment filled with possibilities and potential. ***Embrace it with curiosity and an open mind***. The path ahead is uniquely yours to shape!

1

Beating Procrastination

"Procrastination makes easy things hard and hard things harder."

Mason Cooley

You're sitting at your desk with a blank page staring back at you while the clock ticks loudly in the background. You want to get your work done, but there are so many other things to do, like watch TV, check social media, or even clean your room. This is classic procrastination, a habit that sneaks up on you when you least expect it.

This chapter will help you understand why it happens and how to overcome it. We'll explore the psychological triggers that make procrastination so easy and explore ways to beat it.

1.1 Understanding the Root Causes of Procrastination

Procrastination typically results from psychological triggers that prevent you from getting started. For many, fear of failure causes a mental block. Thinking about failure can paralyze you, making it easy to delay tasks instead of hunkering down to get assignments done.

Perfectionism fuels procrastination when the desire to be flawless stops you from ever starting a project. You could get caught in an endless loop of planning and preparation, never feeling ready enough to start. Worse, lack of motivation can sap your energy, making it difficult to muster the will to take the first step.

Decision fatigue is another culprit in the procrastination puzzle. Making countless decisions every day, from what to wear to what to eat, can exhaust your mental resources. This type of fatigue leads to avoidance behavior when your brain seeks to conserve energy by delaying further decision-making. After a long day of choices, deciding how to approach a complex project can be overwhelming, leading you to set it aside for later. This can create a vicious cycle, where the longer you delay decisions, the more daunting they appear.

Task aversion plays a significant role in procrastination. Tasks that are unpleasant or daunting are easy to avoid. The thought of tackling a mountain of paperwork or starting an intense study session can lead to indefinite postponement. However, breaking tasks into smaller manageable parts can make them less intimidating. Focus on one step at a time to reduce the overwhelming nature of the task and progress without being bogged down by its enormity.

Anxiety often accompanies procrastination, where it becomes a habit. Anxiety can magnify the fear of starting or finishing a task, leading to procrastination as a coping method. Fretting over anxiety can be paralyzing, making you avoid tasks altogether. To counter this, techniques like mindfulness and deep breathing can help manage anxiety-related procrastination. By calming your mind and focusing on the moment, you can loosen the grip of anxiety and regain focus on the task at hand.

Reflection Section

Take a moment to reflect on your procrastination experiences. *What psychological triggers do you recognize in yourself?*

- Think about times when fear of failure or decision fatigue held you back. Jot down a few instances and think about how you felt then.
- Awareness is the first step to understanding your procrastination habits and taking control of them.
- Identifying those patterns can empower you to address them proactively to pave the way for a productive and fulfilling life.

Step	Details
Task to Complete	Write down the specific task you've been procrastinating on.
Apply the Pomodoro Technique	Commit to working on the task for 25 minutes.
Break Task into Smaller Steps	List the steps needed to complete the task, in order of priority.
Find an Accountability Partner	Name someone who will help keep you on track through regular check-ins.
Reward Yourself	Describe the reward you'll give yourself for completing the task.

1.2 Practical Strategies to Combat Procrastination

The **Pomodoro** technique is noted for its simplicity and effectiveness in terms of productivity. (*Pomodoro is tomato in Italian.*) Picture yourself setting a dedicated time of 25 minutes for focused work where distractions are not allowed. *Francesco Cirillo* developed this method to help you concentrate on one task at a time, breaking work into manageable intervals. After each session, you reward yourself with a short break to rest and recharge your mind. The cycle repeats, creating a rhythm to enhance concentration and productivity. The beauty of the Pomodoro technique is its ability to make daunting tasks less overwhelming since you only need to commit to 25 minutes at a time. This is a small commitment with a significant impact on gradually building momentum to reduce procrastination.

Beyond techniques, ***setting clear goals*** is fundamental to maintaining focus and motivation. Specific, measurable objectives provide roadmaps to guide you through tasks with clear understanding. For example, if you're planning a trip, you wouldn't just set off in your car without a destination in mind. Similarly, having clear goals keeps you on track.

- Break your tasks into bite-sized portions to bring hasten completion.
- Prioritize tasks based on their deadlines to ensure that the most urgent tasks are tackled first.
- This structured approach prevents being overwhelmed because you can focus on one step at a time, knowing exactly what needs to be done and when.

Accountability adds another layer of motivation. Partner with a friend or colleague with similar productivity goals to yield big benefits. Regular check-ins via text or in person create a sense of responsibility. This is like having a buddy encouraging you to hit the gym even when your energy is low. Knowing that someone else is keeping track of your progress pushes you to stay committed. Such partnerships foster supportive environments by sharing struggles and celebrating victories to make the process enjoyable and less isolating.

Motivation tends to wane, but there are strategies to reignite it. Set up a reward system for yourself. When you finish a challenging task, treat yourself to something you enjoy, like a favorite snack or a short break to watch a funny video. Positive reinforcement links task completion with pleasure, making it easier to finish future hurdles. Visualization is another powerful tool. Think of yourself completing a task and the satisfaction that follows. Imagine the relief and accomplishment you'll feel when it's done. Mental imagery can boost your drive by transforming a mundane task into something you're eager to complete.

Exercise: Create a Procrastination-Busting Plan

- Take a moment to outline a strategy to fight procrastination.
- Write down a task you've been putting off.
- Apply the Pomodoro technique by setting a timer for 25 minutes and commit to that amount of focused work time.
- Break the task into smaller steps, noting them in order of priority.
- Find an accountability partner and agree on regular check-ins.

- Last, select a reward you'll give yourself once the task is complete.
- Keep the plan visible, such as a sticky note on your desk to remind you of your commitment and the steps you'll take to overcome procrastination.

Reflection Prompt	Your Thoughts
Psychological Triggers	What triggers procrastination for you? (e.g., fear of failure, decision fatigue, etc.)
Specific Instances	Describe moments when procrastination held you back.
Feelings Experienced	How did you feel during these moments? (e.g., anxious, overwhelmed, indifferent, etc.)
Patterns Observed	What recurring patterns do you notice in your procrastination habits?
Steps to Address Them	How can you proactively address these triggers in the future?

1.3 Digital Tools to Boost Your Productivity

In the digital age, technology is an ally in your quest for productivity. Technology is like a personal assistant who keeps track of your tasks and deadlines and even helps you focus. That's the magic of productivity apps.

- **Todoist** is an example, a tool that transforms task management into an intuitive experience. It organizes tasks into projects, sets priorities, and even shares tasks with collaborators. Todoist is like a digital checklist to remind you what to do next to keep tasks categorized to make tackling them one by one easier.
- **Trello** uses a visual approach to turn projects into cards on a board if you plan projects. Think of it as a digital bulletin board where you can drag tasks from to-do to done by

visually tracking progress. This method lets you see the bigger picture without losing sight of the details. It's especially helpful when you're juggling multiple projects or working on a team so everyone can see what's happening in real-time. Trello is an organized, transparent way to manage your projects and stay on top of everything easily.
- Focusing in a world full of distractions is challenging, but apps like **Forest** make it more engaging. Forest uses a gamified approach to help maintain focus. Every time you need to concentrate, you plant a virtual tree. The tree grows as you work, but if you leave the app, the tree dies. It's a simple, effective way to encourage focus, and over time, you'll see your forest flourish as a visual testament to your productivity. It's a small incentive that can keep you on track.
- Digital calendars are another tool to streamline your schedule. **Google Calendar** offers features like reminders, event notifications, and the ability to share your calendar with others. You can sync it across devices so you're always up to date, no matter where you are. The digital calendar acts as a central hub for your life to organize everything from meetings to personal commitments. The convenience of having your schedule at your fingertips, knowing that your schedule is set each day with times and locations.
- Time-tracking applications like **Toggl** track how your time is spent. By logging work hours, you can identify peak productivity times, discover where time slips away, and adjust your schedule accordingly. It's like having a mirror to view your daily habits to help you make decisions about

allocating your time effectively. Tracking time might seem tedious at first, but the insights you gain are invaluable to optimize your workflow.

- Automation tools, such as **IFTTT** (if this, then that), are designed to minimize repetitive tasks. Set simple triggers and actions to automate everyday tasks like saving email attachments to cloud storage or posting updates across multiple social media platforms. Automation saves time and reduces mental clutter so that one can focus on tasks that require more brainpower. This is like having a smart helper to ensure that mundane tasks are taken care of so you can dedicate your time and energy where you need them.

Tool Name	Purpose	Key Features
Todoist	Task Management	Organize tasks into projects, set priorities, share tasks, and track deadlines.
Trello	Visual Project Planning	Use boards and cards to organize tasks, track progress visually, and collaborate in real-time.
Forest	Focus Enhancement	Gamify focus by planting virtual trees that grow as you concentrate; lose focus, and the tree dies.
Google Calendar	Schedule Management	Set reminders, get notifications, share calendars, and sync across devices.
Toggle	Time Tracking	Log work hours, analyze productivity patterns, and optimize time allocation.
IFTTT	Task Automation	Automate repetitive tasks using customizable triggers and actions.

1.4 Designing a Personal Productivity System

Visualize a one-size-fits-all outfit intended to fit everyone. While it may fit some people, for most, it's either too tight or too loose in places. Productivity systems are similar, where what works wonders for one person might not fit others at all. That's why having a tailored productivity system is crucial to see your unique strengths and weaknesses and design a system to complement them.

- First, understand when you feel most energized.

Are you a morning person, or do you thrive in the quiet of the night? Understanding your natural rhythms can guide you to a routine that maximizes productivity.

- Establishing a daily routine begins with morning rituals that set the tone for the rest of the day. Maybe you do stretches or enjoy quiet time with a cup of coffee or a quick review of your goals. Rituals create a sense of readiness and focus by jotting down tomorrow's tasks or spending time to reflect on what went well that day. Such practices are flexible and adaptable to your needs as they change.
- Your environment is important for your productivity. A cluttered workspace often leads to a cluttered mind. Organizing your desk and keeping items in designated spots to keep mental space clear, allowing better focus. Think of the things that enhance your concentration. This could be a certain type of lighting, background music, or complete silence. A plant or two brings a touch of nature indoors. Tailor your space to suit your preferences and create an atmosphere you enjoy that encourages focus and creativity.
- Evaluate and adjust your productivity system regularly, which is as important to track your progress and patterns that you notice. It doesn't have to be a detailed account but

rather a place to jot down what works and what doesn't. Set monthly review sessions with yourself to review the information. *Are there adjustments that could increase efficiency?*

A new tool or method might be worth trying. These evaluations are opportunities to reset, ensuring that your system evolves with you.

Visual Element: Productivity Check-In Chart

Create a simple chart with two columns:

1. *What's Working*
2. *What Needs Tweaking*

Week of: _____

What's Working ✓	What Needs Tweaking ⚡
1. _____	1. _____
2. _____	2. _____
3. _____	3. _____
4. _____	4. _____
5. _____	5. _____

Review Date: _____

Reminder: Small steps lead to big changes. Keep this chart visible and update it weekly.

At the end of each week, spend a few minutes filling it out. The chart will be a visual snapshot of progress and improvement areas to help you make sound decisions about your productivity system.

- Keep it in a visible spot as a gentle reminder that productivity is an ongoing process. Visual reminders can be powerful tools for focus and motivation to guide and motivate you as you manage tasks and goals.

1.5 Embracing Progress Over Perfection

Striving for perfection is a noble pursuit, but it can lead to stagnation and procrastination. When you set the bar impossibly high, fear of not measuring up can prevent you from taking any action at all. You might find yourself endlessly tweaking a project without finishing it because it doesn't meet your exacting standards. The pursuit of flawlessness can paralyze, causing stress and delaying progress.

Recognizing a tendency toward perfectionism is the first step in freeing yourself from it. First, identify times when you're stuck—not because the task is difficult, but because you're afraid it won't be perfect. Imperfection is a natural part of growth that helps you move forward when things aren't flawless. Realize that progress matters most, not perfection.

A ***growth mindset*** shifts focus from results to learning and improving. This mindset encourages viewing challenges as opportunities for development rather than threats to your self-worth. Celebrating small victories along the way reinforces positive behavior and builds momentum. Each step forward, no matter how minor, is a step toward your goals. Embracing progress is the partner of the learning process rather than fixating on unattainable ideals. This perspective nurtures resilience and adaptability, which are key traits in managing life's complexities.

To **overcome perfectionism**, first set realistic expectations. Instead of aiming for an impeccable outcome, aim for completion instead. The first draft doesn't have to be perfect; it just has to happen. This approach reduces pressure and makes starting a task less daunting. Learn from mistakes rather than fearing them. Mistakes aren't failures; they're valuable lessons that guide you to better results. Reflect on what didn't work and why, then adjust your approach. This is an iterative process leading to continuous improvement and greater satisfaction in your work.

Self-compassion is vital to combat perfectionism. Be kind to yourself, especially during setbacks. Treat yourself with the same understanding and patience you would offer a friend facing similar challenges. Recognize that everyone experiences difficulties that don't define your worth. Practicing self-compassion fosters resilience to bounce back from disappointments with fresh determination to grow and embrace success and failure. Remind yourself that each experience (good or bad) contributes to personal development.

As you embrace ***progress over perfection***, remember that your worth is not defined by flawless achievements and your willingness to learn and grow. By shifting focus from perfection to progress, you open to new possibilities and reduce the paralysis resulting from unattainable goals. Celebrate each small victory, learn from every misstep, and treat yourself with kindness to enhance productivity and enrich your life for more fulfillment and rewards. Moving forward, remember that growth and learning shape you and who you will become.

With each step, you grow, evolve, and create a truly meaningful life.

1.6 Transform with Cognitive Restructuring

Cognitive Restructuring, a fundamental technique of cognitive-behavioral therapy, was pioneered by psychiatrist Aaron T. Beck in the 1960s. Initially aimed at treating depression, Beck found that changing negative and distorted thought patterns could significantly improve patients' emotions and behaviors. This approach has evolved to address various psychological challenges, proving especially effective in overcoming procrastination and boosting productivity by transforming obstructive thoughts into proactive ones.

Step 1: Identify Limiting Thoughts

Observe the moments when procrastination creeps in, and pinpoint the thoughts that accompany it. You might find yourself thinking:

- "I can start this later."
- "I'm not ready to tackle this yet."
- "This is too complicated right now."

Step 2: Question Your Initial Thoughts

Challenge these procrastination-driven thoughts to test their accuracy and helpfulness. Reflect on questions like:

- "Are these thoughts factual, or are they driven by my emotions?"
- "What proof do I have that supports or disputes these thoughts?"

- "What are the repercussions if I follow these thoughts and delay my task?"

This step is crucial for dismantling the irrational beliefs that justify procrastination.

Step 3: Reformulate Thoughts

Replace your initial, unhelpful thoughts with ones that promote action and resolve. Transform them into empowering mantras:

- "Starting small now will pave the way for easier steps later."
- "There's no better time than now to get going."
- "I just need to take the first step; perfection can wait."

Step 4: Visualize the Outcome

Imagine the satisfaction and relief of completing your task. How will you feel? What benefits will you reap? Visualization can significantly amplify your motivation and drive to commence and persist with your work.

Step 5: Practice Regularly

Regular practice of Cognitive Restructuring makes it a natural part of your problem-solving toolkit. The more you practice, the more second nature it becomes, helping to reduce procrastination and boost your productivity over time.

By adopting Cognitive Restructuring, you turn the daunting task of starting into a series of manageable, rational steps. This method not only aids in overcoming the immediate hurdle of procrastination but also cultivates a resilient mindset for enduring productivity improvements. This technique proves that a thoughtful reconsideration of our thoughts can lead to powerful shifts in our behavior, making it easier to start and finish tasks with confidence and clarity.

2

Mastering Time Management

"The key is not to prioritize what's on your schedule, but to schedule your priorities."

Stephen Covey

See yourself staring at a to-do list that seems to grow longer by the hour. Each task competes for your attention, demanding to be prioritized, but you're not sure where to start. You might feel like you're spinning plates to keep everything balanced without crashing to the ground. It's a familiar scene for many young adults, often juggling A to Z responsibilities from academics to work, social engagements, and personal goals. This chapter will help you manage the chaos and introduce you to ways to manage your time.

2.1 Prioritize Tasks With the Eisenhower Box

One of the most effective tools to prioritize tasks is the **Eisenhower Box**. Named after *Dwight D. Eisenhower*, who famously used this method to prioritize his Eisenhower Matrix duties, this tool helps you sort tasks by urgency and importance. Divide your tasks into four distinct quadrants.

- The *first quadrant* is for urgent and important tasks, like the fire alarm, that demand immediate attention and action. Another example might be an assignment due tomorrow or a meeting with your boss.
- The *second quadrant* represents important but not urgent tasks. These are stepping stones to long-term goals, such as planning a major project or setting aside time for professional development. These tasks require thought and consideration but don't demand immediate action.
- The *third quadrant* is for tasks that are urgent but not important. These often include interruptions that demand your attention but don't contribute to your long-term objectives, like some emails or phone calls, and daily chores that can be delegated to others. The idea here is to minimize time spent on these activities or delegate them when possible to focus on more impactful tasks.
- Finally, the *fourth quadrant* contains tasks that are neither urgent nor important. These are typically activities that offer little to no value, such as mindlessly scrolling through social media or engaging in busy work that could be eliminated from your schedule. The recommendation for these tasks is to eliminate them as much as possible to make room for tasks in the other three quadrants that align more closely with your goals and priorities.

Urgent & Important	Not Urgent & Important
Do these tasks now.	Schedule these tasks.
Urgent & Not Important	**Not Urgent & Not Important**
Delegate these tasks.	Eliminate these tasks.

To effectively categorize tasks using the Eisenhower Box, start with a daily assessment to list everything you need to accomplish.

- Sort each task into one of the four quadrants. This practice clarifies what needs immediate attention and highlights where you should invest your time for future gains.
- At the end of the week, conduct a planning session.
- Review your tasks and outcomes, adjusting priorities as necessary.
- A weekly evaluation keeps you aligned with your goals, ensuring that important tasks don't fall by the wayside in favor of the urgent.

The benefits of the Eisenhower Box are numerous. By categorizing tasks, you reduce the overwhelm from a seemingly endless list of to-dos. This method increases focus on critical tasks, allocating time and energy where they matter most. Instead of jumping from task to task, concentrate on completing the ones that match with your long-term objectives for sustained progress and success.

Practical examples illustrate this, such as responding to work emails that fall into the urgent/important quadrant, requiring your immediate attention to keep work running smoothly. In contrast, planning a long-term project might fit into the important but not urgent quadrant. This is an investment in future successes with thoughtful planning and time to develop thoroughly.

Reflection Section

Reflect on your current approach to task management. *How often do you react to urgent demands instead of moving steadily toward your goals?*

- Plan to spend time each week to create an Eisenhower Box for upcoming tasks.
- Note the balance between urgent and important tasks and adjust your schedule to dedicate time to the tasks that drive your long-term success.
- Reflection can be a powerful exercise to shift your focus from basic day-to-day survival to actively building your desired future.

	Urgent	**Not Urgent**
Important	**DO FIRST**	**SCHEDULE**
	• Crisis management	• Strategic planning
	• Deadline-driven projects	• Relationship building
	• Emergency meetings	• Personal development
	• Last-minute preparations	• Exercise and health
	Handle these immediately	*Set specific time to do these*
Not Important	**DELEGATE**	**ELIMINATE**
	• Interruptions	• Time wasters
	• Some calls/emails	• Excessive social media
	• Some meetings	• Busy work
	• Popular activities	• Pleasant distractions
	Find someone to do these	*Minimize or eliminate these*

2.2 Time Blocking: A Guide to Maximizing Your Day

When you schedule time for the important things you need to do every day, you're in control, and stress is minimized. This is the beauty of time blocking, a technique that turns your schedule into a series of intentionally focused segments. Allocating time for specific tasks helps you create a structured day with maximized efficiency. Instead of juggling multiple responsibilities at once, you dedicate attention to one task at a time, avoiding the pitfalls of multitasking that often lead to mistakes and fatigue. Time blocking transforms chaos into order, where each task has its own place without competing for your attention.

- To implement time blocking effectively, identify when you're most productive. Everyone has those golden hours when they're most energetic and focused. For some, it's early morning, while others hit their stride late in the afternoon. Once you've pinpointed your peak productivity hours, use them for your most demanding tasks.
- Next, schedule regular breaks and leisure activities. Breaks are vital pauses to recharge your mind and keep burnout at bay. Consider scheduling time for a walk, quick meditation, or simply stepping away from your desk. The goal is to create a balanced day of productivity and well-being.
- Time blocking offers numerous advantages, chiefly enhanced focus and productivity. Dedicating time to tasks reduces the mental clutter that comes from trying to do everything at once. A structured approach allows you to immerse yourself in each task, leading to higher-quality work and a satisfying sense of accomplishment. Time blocking can also significantly improve work-life balance

by setting clear boundaries between work and personal time so you're not working late at night when you should be unwinding.
- However, time blocking isn't without its challenges. Interruptions are inevitable from unexpected meetings or urgent requests. The key is building flexibility into your schedule to allocate buffer times between blocks to accommodate unforeseen demands. This way, a sudden change won't derail your entire day. Also, be open to adjusting your blocks as needed. If you find that a task takes longer than expected, don't stress. Extend the block or move less critical tasks to another time. Remember, the purpose of time blocking is to empower you, not to confine you to a rigid schedule.
- Time blocking takes practice and extra effort at the start, but it eventually leads to a more organized, fulfilling day. You'll likely achieve more in less time when each task gets the focused attention it deserves. This method helps you manage current responsibilities and allows you to carve out time for new opportunities and growth. Plan each day with time blocks and note how moving from task to task can be done purposefully and how it could change your perspective when your time is maximized.

2.3 Digital Detox: Reclaiming Your Time From Screens

In today's digital landscape, screens often dominate life. From the moment you wake up until you fall asleep, you're likely tethered to a device, whether a phone, laptop, or tablet. While technology undoubtedly offers convenience and connection, it can also be distracting.

- Excessive screen time can affect your ability to focus, leading to a reduced attention span. You've probably noticed how easy it is to lose track of time scrolling through social media or binge-watching your favorite show, later realizing that precious time has been squandered.
- The constant barrage of digital stimuli can affect stress levels. The pressure to keep up, respond immediately, and keep up can create a mental load that leads to stress.
- Give yourself a moment to breathe without the relentless ping of distracting notifications.

Enter the concept of digital detox—a deliberate effort to unplug devices and reconnect with the real world around you. Think of it as a reset button for your brain and a chance to clear mental cobwebs and regain clarity. By stepping away from screens, even briefly, you re-engage with offline activities that digital demands can overshadow. Enjoy the simplicity of reading a book, where the only notifications come from you turning pages, or the creativity that flows when you pick up a paintbrush or tend a garden. Those activities ground you and nourish your mental well-being. Think of them as a refuge from constant digital noise.

Digital detox doesn't mean abandoning technology altogether; it's a matter of balance. Set aside tech-free time in your day whenever it's convenient. Use this time to engage in mindful, enjoyable activities that don't depend on screens. Perhaps a morning walk when it's relatively peaceful or an evening spent journaling your thoughts.

These practices help to cultivate a sense of peace and presence, allowing you to disconnect from the digital world and reconnect with yourself. Consider a tech-free zone in your living space, an area where devices aren't allowed, where you unwind without digital interference.

There's a plethora of alternatives to screen time, each with unique benefits. You might dive into a novel, gather dust on a shelf and lose yourself in the story, or channel your inner artist by exploring painting, drawing, or any creative hobby that interests you.

- Gardening is a wonderful, relaxing way to disconnect by nurturing plants that feed both soul and body.
- A leisurely stroll in a nearby park contributes to digital detox, where you can relax, breathe, and observe the world at your own pace.

These activities remind you that the richness of life doesn't exist solely on a screen. Allow yourself moments of offline engagement to reclaim useful time and rediscover the joys of living fully in the moment.

2.4 Setting Boundaries to Protect Your Time

What if time is a finite resource constantly tugged in different directions by friends, work, school, and other commitments? Without clear boundaries, this precious resource can quickly be depleted, leaving you stretched thin and overwhelmed.

Setting time boundaries is crucial to maintaining life balance, which is protecting your time from being consumed by responsibilities that may not fit your priorities. You might have to decline extra work to focus on your studies or block off time every week to pursue a hobby that brings you joy and prevents burnout. There is no guilt in setting limits to conserve energy for things that truly matter to you.

Establishing time boundaries begins with *communication.* Politely declining new responsibilities is an important skill that protects your time. Prioritizing your own needs and commitments is essential to your health, well-being, and balance. When someone requests your time, consider whether the request aligns with your goals. If it doesn't, explain your situation clearly and offer an alternative.

Scheduling *personal time* is another effective strategy. Treat those blocks of time as you would any other commitment—non-negotiable and essential for your well-being. This could be regular time with friends or simply time for rest and relaxation. Make appointments with yourself to reinforce their importance, ensuring other obligations don't push them aside.

Maintaining boundaries can be challenging. You might face pressure from others to bend your schedule or feel guilty about protecting your time. Remember that your time is valuable, and protecting it is a form of *self-respect*. If you're pressured, remember your priorities and the reasons you set boundaries in the first place.

Managing guilt or saying no doesn't make you selfish; it means you're mindful of your limits. You have the authority to prioritize your needs without feeling obligated to meet the expectations of others. This mindset shift empowers you to consistently uphold your boundaries for a healthy life balance.

The benefits of firm time boundaries are substantial. You'll likely find that your productivity increases as you focus intently on the most important tasks. Minimize activities that drain your energy and preserve space for fulfilling and satisfying pursuits. Protected personal time enhances your well-being, allowing you to recharge, reduce stress, and maintain control of your life.

With solid boundaries, you're better equipped to handle modern life demands with harmony between commitments and aspirations. Remember that boundaries enhance your ability to say ***yes to yourself.***

2.5 The Art of Saying No: Protect Your Priorities

If you look at your life like a canvas, each commitment can be thought of as a brushstroke shaping the picture of your day. For many, the canvas becomes cluttered with strokes of obligations that don't contribute to the masterpiece you envision. Saying no is like choosing the right colors, where each one contributes to the overall beauty and balance of your life. No is sometimes essential for effective time management, allowing you to focus on what truly matters. By declining non-essential commitments, you preserve time for important tasks and avoid the over-commitment trap. Prioritizing personal goals is feasible when you have space to breathe and think clearly about what matches your aspirations.

Yet saying no isn't always easy. It requires a blend of assertiveness and tact to decline requests without damaging the relationships you value. If you have to decline, use firm and polite language. You might say, "*I appreciate your offer, but I have other commitments right now.*" Whenever possible, offer alternative solutions or compromises to soften the blow.

For example, if you can't accept a project, suggest someone else who might be able to help or revisit the request at a later time. These strategies communicate respect and consideration, maintain relationships, and protect your time.

Psychological barriers can stand in the way of saying no. Many people fear disappointing others or worry about disapproval. The desire for acceptance can lead to saying yes to everything, even at the expense of your well-being. Overcoming such barriers is recognizing your time as valuable, where declining a request doesn't diminish your worth or kindness. Think about why you hesitate to say no. *Is it FOMO (fear of missing out) or being seen as unhelpful?* Understanding such motivations empowers you to make decisions that honor your boundaries, not the expectations of others.

Recall real-life scenarios when saying no, which leads to successful time management. Think of a student who declines an extra work project to study for upcoming exams. By prioritizing academic goals, you give your best effort where it counts the most. You might limit social obligations or forego a weekend trip to stay home and recharge. Choices allow you to honor responsibilities with fresh energy and focus. These examples illustrate that saying no isn't wrong, but about choosing the doors to open that fit your values and goals.

As you navigate the complexities of modern life, remember that saying no is an affirmation of your priorities. This is a skill you learn to craft a life that matches your aspirations. Setting clear boundaries protects your time to build a foundation for personal and professional success.

This chapter has explored tools and techniques to effectively manage time, preparing you to embrace opportunities ahead. Next, we'll delve into decision-making and problem-solving skills to equip you with strategies to tackle challenges with confidence and clarity.

3

Decision-Making and Problem-Solving Skills

"In any moment of decision, the best thing you can do is the right thing. The worst thing you can do is nothing."

Theodore Roosevelt

When you're at a life crossroad, every path can lead to a different future. Your choice and the weight of the decision press heavily on your shoulders. This is a familiar feeling that many young adults encounter as they learn the complexities of modern life. Whether choosing a career path, deciding where to live, or understanding personal relationships, your ability to make informed, confident decisions is critical. This chapter explores the tools and framework to guide you through those pivotal times and to align choices with your values and aspirations.

3.1 Decision-Making Frameworks for Important Life Choices

In the realm of decision-making, systems like **SWOT** analysis and listing pros and cons are valuable tools. SWOT stands for *Strengths*, *Weaknesses*, *Opportunities*, and *Threats*. This is a structured approach to evaluate options. Identifying internal strengths and weaknesses, along with external opportunities and threats, yields a comprehensive view of each situation. This is an analytical process to help you make balanced decisions by evaluating potential benefits and risks.

On the other hand, a pros-and-cons list is a straightforward way to analyze options. List the advantages and disadvantages of each choice to create a visual picture that simplifies complex decisions. Clarity is particularly helpful when you're faced with equally attractive alternatives, allowing you to see the options that best align with your goals.

- *Aligning decisions with personal values* is another key aspect of effective decision-making. Your values are the guiding principles that shape your identity and influence your actions. When decisions reflect core beliefs, they resonate with authenticity and fulfillment. To identify your personal values, consider what matters most. It could be family, career success, creativity, or adventure. Once you've pinpointed values, ensure that your decisions support your long-term aspirations. Alignment enhances satisfaction and provides a compass to navigate the uncertainties in life. Stay true to yourself to create a meaningful, purposeful life.
- *Prioritizing decisions* is another skill that greatly enhances effectiveness. Not all decisions carry the same weight;

understanding them requires time and resources. It's important to distinguish between urgent and important decisions. Urgent decisions demand immediate attention, while important ones contribute to long-term goals. The Eisenhower Matrix mentioned in previous chapters is useful for setting priorities. Categorizing decisions based on urgency and importance allows focus on efforts that matter most to avoid getting caught up in trivial matters.

The role of research- and information-gathering cannot be overstated when it comes to making informed decisions.

In today's information-rich world, the ability to sift through data for relevant insights is invaluable. Conduct thorough research to understand the nuances of your options by reading articles, consulting experts, and/or reading case studies. Ensure that the sources you rely on are credible and trustworthy, as misinformation can lead to misguided choices. Arm yourself with the knowledge to gain confidence to make informed, intentional decisions that pave the way to success in important life aspects.

Reflection Section

- Think about a recent decision you made and reflect on the process you used.

  How could a decision-making framework have influenced the outcome?
  What values were in play, and how did they guide your choices?

- Take time to jot down your thoughts, identifying areas where you felt strong and where you might improve. Reflection is a step toward refining decision-making skills to ensure that future choices match your goals and values.

- *Describe the recent decision you made.*

....

- *What process did you use to make the decision?*

....

- *How might a decision-making framework have helped?*

....

- *What values influence your choice?*

....

- *Where did you feel confident in the process?*

....

- *What aread could you improve in?*

....

3.2 Problem-Solving Techniques for Everyday Challenges

On a typical day with a problem that feels like a roadblock, such as an unexpected schedule glitch that made you decide between attending a critical meeting or catching up on overdue assignments. Perhaps there's a misunderstanding in a group project where everyone seems to be on a different page, causing friction and delays. These are everyday challenges that can be daunting, but a structured problem-solving approach can make a world of difference.

- First, identify the root cause by digging deeper and wondering why until you uncover the underlying factors. Once you know what's truly at play, brainstorm potential solutions. Don't limit yourself at this stage; let your ideas flow freely and consider even seemingly outlandish ones.
- After generating a list of possibilities, evaluate and select the best solution. Look at each option critically, weighing the pros and cons. Consider feasibility, required resources, and the potential outcomes of each choice.
- Once you've settled on a solution, implement it with confidence. This is where the rubber meets the road, turning plans into action. But don't stop there. Review solution effectiveness, assessing whether it resolved the issue or if adjustments are needed. The cycle of action and reflection ensures consistent strengthening of problem-solving skills that are ready to tackle the next challenge with greater ease.

Creative thinking plays a pivotal role here, encouraging you to think outside the box and explore innovative solutions. Mind mapping is a powerful technique to aid exploration. Visually organize your thoughts to uncover connections and possibilities that aren't immediately apparent. Encouraging diverse perspectives is also valuable. When you face a problem, seek input from others who might see things differently. Their insights can spark new ideas and lead to solutions you haven't considered. This is a collaborative approach that enriches the problem-solving process and fosters an environment of thriving creativity.

Consider a scenario where you manage time conflicts between work and studies. You might view this initially as a simple scheduling issue, but applying a structured problem-solving approach helps you dig deeper. Perhaps the root cause is a lack of prioritization or inefficient time management.

- By brainstorming solutions, you might discover a new way to organize tasks by allocating specific times for focused work and study. Similarly, resolving misunderstandings in group projects often requires addressing communication gaps.
- By fostering open dialogue and actively listening to each team member, you can create a collaborative atmosphere that encourages ongoing cooperation and clarity.

Persistence and adaptability are key when initial solutions don't pan out as expected. Not every approach works perfectly on the first try, and that's okay. The important thing is to remain resilient and willing to iterate on solutions. If one strategy fails, analyze why and adapt or adjust your approach. This could mean pivoting to a different tactic or refining methods to better suit the situation. The willingness to learn from setbacks and adjust accordingly ultimately leads to success. As you continue navigating life's challenges, remember that each problem is an opportunity to grow and develop skills that equip you for whatever comes next.

3.3 Overcoming Indecisiveness: Gaining Confidence in Your Choices

There are times in life when you're faced with a simple task, yet you feel overwhelmed by all the options (cereal, for example). This everyday scenario reflects a deeper challenge many face: indecisiveness. The ***fear of making the wrong choice*** can be paralyzing, leading to a cycle of second-guessing and hesitation. Instead of moving forward, you're stuck analyzing every possible outcome and worrying about the consequences of each decision. It isn't just fear of failure that holds you back; it's also over-reliance on others' opinions. Seeking advice is natural, but when you depend too heavily on external input, you can lose touch with your own instincts. Dependence can cloud your judgment, leaving you unsure of what you truly want.

- Decision-making confidence requires trust in your own judgment. One effective strategy is ***setting a deadline to decide***. When you give yourself a finite timeline, you reduce the tendency to overthink, forcing yourself to make a choice. Choosing can alleviate anxiety resulting from prolonged deliberation and allows decision-making with conviction.
- Another helpful technique is ***limiting the options you consider.*** The paradox of choice suggests that too many options are overwhelming, leading to indecision. By narrowing your choices to a select few, you simplify the process and make it easier to weigh the pros and cons.

Self-awareness is crucial to gaining confidence in your decisions. Reflect on past choices and outcomes.

What patterns do you notice? Are there specific situations where you hesitate more?

Understanding these patterns can help you identify triggers that contribute to indecisiveness. Awareness allows addressing triggers head-on. You might keep a journal to document your decisions and the reasons behind them. Over time, you'll see the progress you've made and develop a clear understanding of your decision-making style. Reflection builds confidence and provides valuable insights into your preferences and values.

Practicing decision-making in low-stakes situations is another way to increase confidence. Everyday scenarios provide ample opportunities to hone this skill. This could be as easy as what to eat for dinner or selecting a movie to watch, but practice making quick decisions and stick with them. Low-pressure choices allow you to practice trusting your instincts without fear of significant consequences.

Utilizing role-playing and decision-making exercises is also beneficial. Decision planning is a mental rehearsal to make decisions you're comfortable with. The more you do it, the easier it is to decide when faced with significant choices.

Indecisiveness is also a common challenge, but it doesn't define your ultimate approach to life. You can overcome hurdles by understanding factors that contribute to indecision and implementing strategies to build confidence. Trust your ability to make sound decisions drawing on your experiences. Embrace making choices big and small to strengthen confidence and pave the way to a more decisive future.

3.4 The Role of Intuition in Decision-Making

You're trying to decide if logic and analysis have taken you as far as they can. This is where intuition whispers, offering guidance, cutting through uncertainty. Intuition is a gut feeling or instinctual insight, powerful yet sometimes overlooked as an ally in decision-making. It operates on a subconscious level, drawing from experience and knowledge you might not even be aware you possess. This is an internal compass to guide you when data is sparse or when choices seem equally weighted, nudging you to paths that resonate with a deeper understanding of yourself.

There are moments when intuition reigns supreme, particularly in decisions where limited data stops at a crossroads. Imagine you're faced with a choice about accepting a job offer. The salary is competitive, and the company has a solid reputation, yet something feels off. In those situations, relying on intuition can be invaluable. It synthesizes your many experiences, from previous workplaces to interactions with colleagues, for a holistic perspective that facts alone might miss. Trust your inner voice to lead you to decisions that align with your values and aspirations, even if they defy conventional logic.

Enhancing intuitive thinking doesn't happen overnight, but there are ways to develop and trust that skill. Mindfulness practices help you tune into your intuition by quieting the noise of daily life and centering your thoughts. Regular meditation or simply taking a few moments to breathe deeply can sharpen your awareness of intuitive nudges. Journaling is another effective technique. Write down intuitive insights as they occur to recognize patterns and gain confidence in your gut feelings. A written record can be a valuable tool to reflect on past decisions and discover the strength of your intuition.

Balancing intuition with rational analysis is where decision-making is nuanced. Intuition serves as a starting point offering initial direction, but it's important not to rely on it alone. Cross-reference intuitive insights with factual data to build comprehensive decision-making. Suppose you're considering a major life change, like moving to a new city. Your gut tells you it's the right move, but analysis of job opportunities, living costs, and lifestyle factors provides a clearer picture. The combination of intuition and logic ensures that your decisions are heartfelt and well-grounded, reducing the risk of impulsive choices based only on emotion.

Understanding when to lean on intuition and when to delve more into rational analysis is a skill honed over time. As you navigate various decisions, you'll find that intuition often speaks in whispers, prompting subtle, significant shifts in perspective. Cultivating and balancing the internal dialogue with concrete information enhances your ability to make choices that feel right and stand up to scrutiny. Harmony with heart and mind leads to insightful decisions that empower you to move forward with clarity.

3.5 Learning From Mistakes: Turning Failures Into Opportunities

Think about a time when things didn't go as planned—a project fell through, a class didn't turn out as expected, or a relationship ended. It's easy to feel defeated and view those setbacks as indicators of personal shortcomings. However, shifting perspective to see failures as valuable learning experiences can transform those times into stepping stones for growth. Consider such times as opportunities for critical analysis. *What factors contributed to the outcome? Was there a lack of preparation or perhaps a communication misunderstanding?* Dissecting the situation, you uncover insights that inform future decisions, reducing the chance of repeated mistakes.

Conducting a post-mortem analysis of failures is vital to this process.

- First, identify contributing factors. *Was there an external influence or an internal oversight?*
- Next, evaluate the impact of your decisions. *How did they affect the outcome?* Reflection allows you to extract lessons by turning failures into sources of knowledge. With understanding, you can approach future challenges with increased awareness and preparedness.

A mindset shift from viewing failure as a dead-end to seeing it as a detour on the path to success empowers you to embrace challenges with resilience and determination.

Resilience is your ally in bouncing back from setbacks by developing a growth mindset, where change is not feared but welcomed as a learning opportunity. Embrace new approaches that lead to unexpected breakthroughs. Innovators like Thomas Edison turned failures into triumphs. Edison famously said, "*I have not failed. I just found 10,000 ways that won't work.*" His persistence led to the invention of the lightbulb, a testament to the power of resilience. Similarly, J.K. Rowling faced hundreds of rejections before *Harry Potter* became a global phenomenon. Those stories remind us that setbacks are not the end but rather part of the journey to success.

Incorporating those lessons into your life requires adaptability. When plans derail, pivoting and embracing change can open new possibilities. Flexibility allows you to navigate uncertainties with confidence, knowing that each experience, positive or negative, contributes to your personal and professional development. Adaptability handles challenges by turning potential failures into opportunities for innovation and creativity.

As you consider those insights, remember that failure isn't a reflection of your worth but a natural part of growth. Each misstep holds valuable lessons waiting to be uncovered. By approaching failures with curiosity and an open mind, you harness the potential to drive transformation. The key is being persistent and viewing setbacks as temporary hurdles on the path to achieving goals.

Through this lens, failure is less daunting, and the pursuit of success is an exciting adventure filled with learning and discovery. With these principles in mind, you're prepared to tackle the next chapter, where we explore the connection between emotional intelligence and building strong relationships to enhance thriving in a complex world.

4

Health and Wellness in a Fast-Paced World

"Wellness is the complete integration of body, mind, and spirit—the realization that everything we do, think, feel, and believe has an effect on our state of well-being."

Greg Anderson

Picture this: your phone buzzes with notifications, assignments pile up, and your calendar is filled with back-to-back commitments. Amidst the chaos, breathing seems like a luxury. But it's precisely in hectic times that self-care is essential. Establishing a daily self-care routine maintains well-being in a world that never seems to slow down. Self-care isn't an indulgence; it reduces stress levels and enhances emotional resilience to help you through ups and downs with a clear mind and a steady heart.

4.1 Establishing a Daily Self-Care Routine

Creating a personalized self-care plan takes your personal needs, preferences, and activities into consideration to deeply nourish you. Maybe you recharge by reading a good book, the steady flow of a morning run, or the creative expression found in painting or playing an instrument. Once you know what replenishes your energy, allocate time for those activities. Treat them as non-negotiable appointments with yourself that are essential to your routine. Dedicated time is a commitment to your well-being, a sanctuary from the demands of everyday life.

Self-care activities cater to wellness, offering unique health benefits. Journaling provides emotional clarity by allowing you to process thoughts and feelings on paper. Find a private space to explore your innermost thoughts without judgment. Another practice is taking mindful showers to focus on the sensations of warm water on your skin, the scent of soap, and the rhythm of your breath for brief meditation amidst daily tasks. Engaging in creative hobbies—drawing, writing, or crafting—can be therapeutic by allowing your mind to wander and explore new ideas or projects.

Flexibility is important for self-care. Life is unpredictable, and your needs might change from week to week. During particularly busy periods, you may need to modify your routine, perhaps shortening activities or combining them with daily tasks. The goal is to adapt self-care practices to fit your current circumstances so they remain a source of support rather than another item on your to-do list. Embrace the ebb and flow, knowing that self-care is a dynamic process that evolves with you.

Reflection Section

Take time to reflect on your current self-care practices. Consider creating a self-care plan that includes these activities, and remember to adjust as your needs change. Reflection can be a first step toward more balanced and fulfilling life practices.

- *What activities genuinely provide peace and joy?*

....

- *Are there areas to allocate more time for self-care?*

....

- *How much time do I currently dedicate to self-care?*

....

- *What areas of self-care could use more attention?*

....

- *What activities can I add to my self-care routine?*

....

- *How will I adjust my self-care plan as my needs change?*

....

4.2 Nutrition on a Budget

Your body is a complex machine that relies on high-quality fuel to function at its best. This is where balanced nutrition steps in, a pivotal role in supporting your physical and mental well-being. Macronutrients are proteins, carbohydrates, and fats—the primary sources of energy that are essential for different functions. Proteins help build and repair tissues, carbohydrates provide quick energy boosts, and fats give long-term energy storage. Vitamins and minerals are needed in smaller amounts, but they're equally crucial. They support immune function, bone health, and mood regulation so your mind and body run smoothly.

Eating healthy without breaking the bank is achievable with a few strategic moves. Start with a grocery list. This helps you avoid impulse purchases that often add unnecessary costs. Focus on staples like grains and legumes you can buy in bulk for savings. These foods are versatile, the foundation of many meals. Another tip is taking advantage of sales, especially on fresh produce. These foods have lower costs and encourage you to incorporate a range of nutrients into your diet. Watch for sales that make a significant difference in your grocery bill.

Meal planning and preparation are effective ways to cut down on food waste to save money. Make a weekly meal plan to buy only what you'll need to reduce the likelihood of buying items that end up unused. Batch cooking is another cost-saving measure. Prepare a large quantity of your favorite dishes and freeze portions for later use. This saves time on busy days and ensures nutritious meals are ready to go, avoiding the temptation of expensive takeout. With a little forethought, these practices make sticking to a budget much easier.

Cooking at home offers many benefits beyond financial savings. Home-cooked meals allow you to control the ingredients to meet your nutritional goals. Simple recipes with affordable ingredients can be delicious and nourishing.

For instance, dishes like vegetable stir-fries or hearty soups are budget-friendly and packed with nutrients. Exploring different cuisines adds variety to your diet, preventing monotony at dinnertime. A variety of cuisines offers unique flavors and nutritional benefits to broaden your palate and enhance your health. Cooking at home is more than a necessity; it transforms meals into an enjoyable and fulfilling part of everyday life.

4.3 Incorporating Exercise into Daily Life

Start your day with a burst of energy when your mind is clear and focused, ready to tackle whatever comes your way. This isn't just a dream—it's what regular physical activity brings to life. Exercise improves cardiovascular health, strengthens your heart and lungs, and provides stamina to keep you going through the busiest days. Beyond physical benefits, exercise enhances mood and mental clarity by releasing endorphins, the body's natural mood lifters, which help to reduce stress and anxiety. A quick workout can transform your outlook, turning a sluggish morning into a productive day.

Fitting exercise into a packed schedule might seem overwhelming, but creative ways to integrate movement into your routine help you feel your best. Consider walking or cycling for short commutes. Not only do you save on transportation costs, but it's also an excellent way to sneak in daily exercise.

If transportation isn't an option, explore quick home workouts with online videos. Those sessions often require little to no equipment, and they fit into a 20-minute break between classes or work tasks, making it easier to stay active without sacrificing time. The key is consistency, ensuring that movement becomes a regular part of your day rather than an occasional activity.

To ***maintain motivation,*** find activities you genuinely enjoy. Exercise shouldn't be a chore. Try dance classes or join a team sport to bring a social element to fitness, making it fun and engaging. Whether it's the rhythm of a Zumba class or the camaraderie of a soccer team, these activities can be exciting ways to keep moving.

If group settings aren't your style, consider outdoor activities like hiking, swimming, or pickleball. These options allow you to connect with nature, offering a refreshing change from indoor workouts. Those activities can be great ways to explore new environments while staying fit.

Setting realistic fitness goals and tracking your progress keeps you motivated and focused. Start by identifying what you want to achieve, which might be running a 5K race, improving flexibility, or simply feeling more energetic. You can use fitness apps or journals to track workouts and progress for a visual reminder of how far you've come. Celebrate milestones and achievements, no matter how small. Each step forward is a victory to reinforce positive habits and encourage continued effort. This approach helps you reach your fitness goals and boosts your confidence, proving that you can accomplish whatever you set your mind to.

4.4 Understanding Sleep and Recovery

When you wake up after a full night's sleep, do you feel rested and ready to take on whatever the day throws at you? Quality sleep plays a vital role in your health and productivity. This is not just about getting enough sleep. During sleep, your body repairs muscles, consolidates memories, and regulates hormones. This is a restorative process impacting cognitive performance, sharpening focus, and boosting problem-solving skills. A good night's sleep also bolsters your immune system, making you less susceptible to illnesses. Without sleep, your brain struggles to function optimally, and even simple tasks feel like monumental challenges.

Establishing a *healthy sleep routine* is crucial for good health. Set a consistent bedtime and wake-up time, even on weekends. This helps regulate your body's internal clock, making it easier to fall asleep and wake up naturally. Create a calming bedtime ritual to signal to your brain that it's time to wind down. This could be reading a book, taking a warm bath, or practicing gentle stretches or meditation. These rituals detach you from the day's stressors and prepare your mind and body for restful sleep.

Sleep deprivation, on the other hand, can creep in unnoticed until you're deep in its clutches. It manifests as constant fatigue, irritability, and trouble concentrating. Recognizing these symptoms early can help you address the deficit before it worsens. If you find yourself sleep-deprived, consider taking short naps during the day, but keep them under 30 minutes to avoid disrupting your nighttime sleep. Catching up on lost sleep might require adjusting your schedule to prioritize rest. Sometimes, it's about making small changes, like reducing late-night screen time or avoiding caffeine in the afternoon.

Rest and recovery extend beyond sleep. They encompass activities that allow your body and mind to rejuvenate. Incorporating active rest like yoga or stretching can enhance flexibility and relieve tension. These practices help maintain a healthy balance, offering a gentle way to stay active without overexerting yourself.

Listening to your body's signals is essential. If you're feeling worn out, it's okay to skip a workout or take a day off. Rest doesn't mean being idle; it's about replenishing your energy in a way that suits your needs. Recognizing when to pause is a skill that complements your fast-paced life, ensuring resilience and readiness to face new challenges.

4.5 Stress Management Techniques

Modern life is full of pressure, deadlines, and the constant ping of phone notifications. It often feels like a relentless sprint, so it's no wonder that stress is a frequent companion. Work and academic pressures can weigh heavily, with expectations to perform at peak levels. Whether you're preparing for exams or meeting job targets, these demands can create a mental load that's hard to shake. Add to that the social obligations of maintaining friendships and the financial pressures of managing tight budgets, and stress quickly becomes a pervasive part of life. Stress isn't just in your mind; it impacts your health, leading to issues like tension headaches, insomnia, and a weakened immune system.

- Finding effective ways to manage stress is crucial for maintaining a sense of balance. One powerful method is ***deep breathing***. It's simple yet profoundly calming, helping to slow your heart rate and clear your mind. Close your eyes, take a deep breath in, hold it for a count of four,

and then release it slowly. This practice can shift your focus away from stressors to the present moment.
- Another effective strategy is ***progressive relaxation***, which involves tensing and then relaxing each muscle group, starting from your toes and working up to your head. This technique can release physical tension, leaving you feeling more relaxed and grounded.
- Engaging in ***hobbies or creative outlets*** offers another escape from stress. Whether it's painting, playing an instrument, or gardening, these activities provide a sense of accomplishment and joy, offering relief from everyday pressures.

Time management is a significant role player in reducing stress, offering ways to organize and prioritize tasks effectively. By planning your day and setting realistic goals, you can allocate time for work, leisure, and rest. Such structure prevents feeling overwhelmed by endless responsibilities.

Creating a to-do list at the start of each day allows you to focus on completing one task at a time. Prioritizing tasks ensures that the most important ones are tackled first, reducing the anxiety of unfinished projects. Breaking larger tasks into smaller, manageable steps makes them less intimidating and more achievable, allowing for steady progress.

Time management isn't just about squeezing the most into each day but finding balance and reducing mental clutter that contributes to stress. Organizing your time effectively creates space for relaxation and personal growth by transforming stress from an uncontrollable force into a manageable part of life.

4.6 Mindfulness Practices

Mindfulness is about being present and fully engaged with the here and now instead of getting lost in thoughts. It's a practice that has become popular for positively impacting stress management. *How often do you find yourself overwhelmed by the noise of life?* That endless stream of thoughts and worries can distract you from what's right in front of you.

Mindfulness invites you to **pause and observe your thoughts without judgment**, allowing you to experience the world with a fresh perspective. When you focus on the present moment, you increase awareness and reduce stress. Think of the difference it could make when you're no longer caught up in overthinking or worrying about what's up next.

This practice doesn't require sitting in silence for hours. It's as simple as paying attention to your breath or sensations in your body. Mindfulness can be practiced anywhere—waiting in line, walking to class, or during a break at work. This is about taking moments throughout the day to ground yourself and notice details you might otherwise overlook.

When you're mindful, you're more likely to **respond to situations with clarity and calmness** rather than reacting on impulse. Heightened awareness can lead to better emotional regulation as you become more attuned to your feelings and address them constructively.

Enhancing emotional regulation through mindfulness brings a sense of balance. When you're in tune with your emotions, you can navigate more effectively, reducing stress and anxiety. It's like having a tool to help you manage your emotional landscape, providing stability even in turbulent times.

If you're faced with a stressful situation, mindfulness allows you to acknowledge your emotions without letting them control you. Instead of being swept away by upsetting emotions, you can choose how to respond with resilience and adaptability in the face of challenges.

Mindfulness also promotes deeper connections with yourself and others. By cultivating presence, you're more likely to listen actively and engage with the people around you. This can expand your relationships as you become more empathetic and understanding.

Savor time truly listening to a friend without distractions or a delicious meal without rushing through it. Mindful moments enrich your experiences to make life more vibrant and fulfilling.

As we explore the interconnectedness of well-being practices, remember that mindfulness weaves through stress management, emotional health, and everyday living. It offers a path to clarity and inner peace with tools to handle the complexities of modern life. Next, we shift our focus to building and maintaining meaningful relationships, another cornerstone of a fulfilling life.

5

Enhancing Emotional and Mental Well-being

"Almost everything will work again if you unplug it for a few minutes, including you."

Anne Lamott

Picture yourself sitting in a bustling café surrounded by chattering friends, the toasting of champagne flutes, and the hum of life swirling about you. Yet amidst this lively scene, your mind feels scattered, jumping from one thought to another like a restless butterfly. This is a common experience when you're juggling the demands of school, work, and social obligations. This type of mental clutter can result in anxiety and feeling overwhelmed.

Enter mindfulness, a practice that offers refuge from the relentless pace of modern life to cultivate mental clarity and reduce stress. Mindfulness is focusing in the moment so you can concentrate and regulate your feelings. This is like pressing a reset button for your mind to bring calm and perspective to chaos.

5.1 Mindfulness and Meditation Techniques

Daily mindfulness doesn't require a complete lifestyle overhaul. Simple practices like mindful breathing can make a significant difference. Pause, close your eyes, and take a deep breath. As you inhale, fill your lungs with air and exhale to release tension everywhere in your body. This exercise anchors you to the present by quieting racing thoughts.

Another technique is *body scan meditation*, where you mentally scan each part of your body from head to toe, noticing any sensations without judgment. This practice brings a deep connection with your physical self for relaxation and awareness.

Meditation is closely related to mindfulness and has genuine benefits for mental health. Regular meditation can reduce symptoms of anxiety and depression, providing a sanctuary of peace in your mind.

- You will enjoy self-awareness, observing thoughts and emotions without getting entangled in them. Sit quietly with your eyes closed and focus on your breathing. If thoughts arise, acknowledge them and gently return to focused breathing. Over time, this practice cultivates peace and compassion for yourself. Meditation is a tool to steer through life challenges with grace and resilience to recharge and reflect.
- If you're new to mindfulness and meditation, resources abound to guide you. Apps like **Headspace**, **Calm** and **Gaia** offer accessible guided sessions that fit easily into

your schedule. These platforms provide various meditations, from beginner-friendly introductions to advanced techniques so that you can tailor them to your needs.
- Online guided meditation sessions are available through platforms like **YouTube** and **Mindvalley** that offer exploration and are often led by experienced practitioners who offer insights into the practice. These resources make it easy to integrate mindfulness into daily life for support and inspiration as you learn and understand meditation through practice.

Reflection Section

- Set aside a few minutes each day to do a mindfulness exercise or meditate.
- Think about how these practices make you feel and their impact on mental clarity and emotional regulation.
- Keep a journal to note observations, and over time, you might discover patterns and preferences that enhance the experience.
- Reflection supports mindfulness and a deeper connection with yourself, encouraging growth and self-discovery.

- *What mindfulness exercise or meditation did I try today?*

....

- *How did I feel during and after the exercise?*

....

- *What impact did it have on my mental clarity?*

....

- *How did it affect my emotional regulation?*

....

- *What patterns or preferences am I noticing over time?*

....

- *How can I enhance my mindfulness practice further?*

....

5.2 Developing Resilience and Coping Skills

Think about the last time life threw you a curveball. Maybe it was an unexpected grade that didn't reflect your hard work or a job opportunity fell through despite your best efforts. Resilience is the ability to bounce back from setbacks to adapt and recover with strength and determination. You'll grow the emotional strength to face adversity without being overwhelmed. In a world full of uncertainties, resilience is your personal armor, helping you steer through challenges and emerge stronger despite adversity.

Building resilience takes practical steps to build on your experience and reflection. Set realistic expectations and goals for yourself, and understand that everything will always go as planned, which is okay. When you embrace a resilient mindset, you reduce the impact of setbacks.

- Break goals down into manageable steps and celebrate each victory as it comes. This will boost your confidence and provide a plan for progress if obstacles arise.
- Practice gratitude and positive thinking are vital components to help you focus on what you have rather than what you lack to cultivate an expectation of abundance. Keep a gratitude journal to recognize the good in each day with a positive outlook that strengthens resilience.

When stress and anxiety are threatened, effective coping mechanisms are invaluable tools. Having a stress management plan is a powerful step forward.

- You might set aside time each day for relaxation with activities that bring joy or simply pause and breathe deeply. Progressive muscle relaxation is another technique to help alleviate stress. By systematically tensing and relaxing each muscle group, you release physical tension and calm your mind. This is a simple practice that can be done anywhere for immediate stress relief. These coping mechanisms are buffers to help you manage stress without being consumed by it.

Real-life examples of resilience can inspire and guide you through your challenges.

Stephen Hawking continued to advance our understanding of the cosmos, authoring critical theories on black holes and the universe despite severe physical limitations imposed by ALS. Hawking's ability to contribute profoundly to science, coupled with his efforts to make complex ideas accessible through books and public speeches, showcases his intellectual resilience and dedication to education.

Elon Musk faced numerous setbacks, including early SpaceX rocket crashes, yet his determination saw him through financial risks and technological failures to revolutionize the automotive and aerospace industries. His story is a testament to the power of relentless innovation and vision, even when faced with skepticism and financial peril, pushing forward to make electric cars and space travel more accessible.

Serena Williams returned to dominate tennis after severe postpartum health complications, consistently challenging racial and gender inequalities within the sport. Her journey highlights not just physical prowess but also a mental fortitude that propels her to fight for equality in tennis, making her a role model for resilience both on and off the court.

Bethany Hamilton became a symbol of incredible determination after returning to professional surfing despite losing her arm in a shark attack at age 13. Her comeback was not just about competing but excelling in the sport, winning national titles, and inspiring countless others with her story. Hamilton's resilience goes beyond personal achievement; she uses her platform to advocate for facing life's challenges with faith and courage, becoming a motivational speaker and author who touches lives worldwide.

Oprah Winfrey overcame a harsh childhood and numerous professional setbacks to build a media empire, using her platform to inspire and empower a global audience. Her influence extends beyond entertainment into philanthropy and advocacy, where she continues to address and support critical social issues, demonstrating profound impact and leadership.

These role models demonstrated resilience with courage and tenacity. Their stories remind us that setbacks are not an end but rather stepping stones to growth and new opportunities.

You can foster resilience by learning from these stories and applying their lessons. Reflect on the challenges you've faced and how you overcame them. *What strategies did you use, and how can they be tailored for your future use?* Reflection builds self-awareness, enabling you to adapt and grow with each experience. Remember, resilience is a skill that develops over time, strengthened by experiences and the choices you make.

5.3 Self-Care for Mental Health

Visualize waking up each morning feeling calm and ready to face the day. This is the power of ***self-care***, a vital practice necessary for maintaining mental health. In the whirlwind of life, it's easy to be so busy you neglect your own needs, letting burnout and fatigue creep in.

Self-care is a protective layer to shield you from pitfalls by strengthening resilience and providing the tools you need to handle stress effectively. Take deliberate steps to nurture mental well-being to be your best self in every aspect of your life.

- Craft a personalized self-care routine, starting with ***introspection.*** Identify activities that bring you genuine joy and relaxation. This could be anything from painting, taking a leisurely walk, or listening to your favorite playlist. The next step is integrating these activities into daily life. Those things signal that you value well-being and self-care as non-negotiable parts of your routine. Allocate specific slots for these activities so they become a

consistent part of your life instead of an occasional indulgence.
- **Physical health** plays a crucial role in self-care as a foundation and a complement to mental well-being. Regular exercise is a powerful mood booster, releasing endorphins that alleviate stress and anxiety. Take a morning jog, enjoy a yoga session or a dance class. Find a physical activity you enjoy and make it a regular part of your week.
- **Balanced nutrition** is equally important. Fueling your body with wholesome foods provides the energy and nutrients needed to support mental clarity and emotional stability. Adequate sleep and rest are the final pieces of the puzzle, giving the mind and body time to recover and recharge. Prioritize a consistent sleep schedule and create a bedtime routine that signals time to wind down.

For those with hectic lifestyles, incorporating self-care can be challenging, but it's feasible with a bit of *creativity*. Start with short, daily self-care practices that fit easily into your routine. This could be as simple as savoring a cup of tea or taking time to stretch between tasks. Regimens of self-care create a buffer against stress.

Another approach is to ***weave self-care into your existing routines***. If you commute, use that time to listen to an audiobook or a podcast that uplifts and inspires. Turn meal prep into a meditative practice by focusing on the textures and aromas of the meal. Viewing everyday activities as part of self-care, you transform them into opportunities for relaxation and rejuvenation.

As you steer through life, remember that self-care is a dynamic practice that evolves with your needs and circumstances. Listen to your body and mind and adjust your self-care routine so it continues to serve you effectively and bring strength and comfort in the ever-changing landscape of life.

5.4 Recognizing When to Seek Help

If you've been feeling down and struggling to find joy in activities that once brought you happiness, you might need additional support. Perhaps you find it difficult to get out of bed, and simple tasks seem overwhelming. Persistent feelings of sadness or hopelessness may be more than temporary. It's critical to recognize when you need additional support. It might be time to seek help if you're having difficulty with daily activities. Suppose you notice a decline in your ability to concentrate. In that case, you have changes in your sleep or appetite, or you feel disconnected from others; these can be indicators that professional support could be beneficial.

Seeking mental health support is a courageous step to healing and growth.

First, seek appropriate mental health professionals to guide you. Look for a counselor, therapist, or psychiatrist for support. Understanding types of therapy helps you choose the right fit. **Cognitive-behavioral therapy (CBT)** is effective in addressing thought patterns that contribute to emotional distress.

Psychodynamic therapy explores past influences on present behavior, while interpersonal therapy focuses on improving relationships and socialization. Each therapy offers unique benefits, and your choice should meet your personal needs and preferences.

The benefits of professional care can be profound. Therapy and counseling provide safe, confidential environments where you can explore your thoughts and feelings without judgment in a space to learn new perspectives and develop coping strategies tailored to your needs. For many, this leads to greater self-awareness and emotional resilience. View therapy as a toolkit of strategies to utilize when faced with challenges. Therapy can help you handle life confidently. Therapy can also foster a sense of validation and understanding that you're not alone in your struggles.

The support of mental health professionals can be a transformative experience with guidance and insight as you work toward a balanced, fulfilling life.

Resources for mental health support are more accessible than ever. Organizations like the **National Institute of Mental Health (NIMH)** and the **Substance Abuse and Mental Health Services Administration (SAMHSA)** offer valuable information and support services. These platforms provide directories of mental health professionals so you can find someone in your area. They also offer resources such as support for substance use or crisis intervention.

Online therapy platforms, like **BetterHelp** or **Talkspace**, provide flexible options with virtual sessions. Those services offer easy connection with a therapist from the comfort of your home, removing barriers like travel or scheduling conflicts.

Seeking help is a sign of strength, not weakness. It shows your commitment to well-being and willingness to take proactive steps to healing. Remember that seeking support is a powerful act of self-care. It acknowledges your needs and addresses them by paving the way for growth and transformation. This chapter has explored the importance of recognizing when to seek help and offers understanding and support. In the next chapter, we'll delve into building and maintaining relationships, a crucial aspect of emotional well-being and personal fulfillment.

6

Building and Maintaining Relationships

"The quality of your life is the quality of your relationships."

Tony Robbins

You're sitting with a friend in a crowded café, surrounded by the hum of conversations and clinking cups. Both of you are scrolling through your phones, absentmindedly listening to each other's comments. This happens all too much in today's digital world, where genuine connection often takes a back seat to an endless stream of notifications. Yet, building and maintaining meaningful relationships is a vital part of life, especially for young adults facing the complexities of college and adulthood. Strong relationships provide support, understanding, and shared experiences that enrich your life in countless ways.

6.1 Communication Techniques for Stronger Connections

Effective communication supports and enhances strong relationships. *Active listening* transforms ordinary interactions into opportunities for a deeper connection. True active listening is paying attention to what someone is saying and grasping the underlying emotions and intentions there. Active listening requires paying close attention, avoiding distractions, and focusing on the speaker. You can show that you're listening by nodding or with verbal affirmations

Reflective listening techniques like paraphrasing or summarizing what you heard demonstrate that you understand their message. Allow the speaker to express themselves without interruption before you respond. This is part of mutual respect and fosters meaningful, empathetic dialogues.

Communication is more than words. *Nonverbal cues*, like body language and facial expressions, play crucial roles in understanding messages. Maintaining eye contact signals attentiveness and sincerity to foster trust and connection. It shows that you're invested in the conversation and value the other person's words and presence.

Understanding gestures and posture also enhances communication. Relaxed body language invites openness and encourages others to share freely, while crossed arms or averted gazes can unintentionally convey disinterest or defensiveness. When you're attuned to nonverbal signals, you can choose words that align with your intentions to create an honest, harmonious exchange.

Clarity and assertiveness are essential for expressing yourself effectively. Using "I" statements is a powerful technique to communicate feelings without blame. Instead of saying, "*You never listen*

to me," try, "*I feel unheard when I speak.*" This approach reduces defensiveness and opens the door to constructive dialogue.

Assertive, respectful dialogue is part of stating your needs clearly and respecting the perspectives of others to foster collaboration and the feelings of others. Respect and clarity strengthen relationships when both parties feel valued and heard.

Empathy is the cornerstone of meaningful connections. It requires stepping into someone else's shoes to see the world from their perspective and acknowledge their feelings without judgment. Empathy bridges gaps and fosters compassion and understanding in relationships.

Active listening and responding with empathy affirm the other person's experiences to create a safe space for vulnerability and trust. An empathetic approach deepens relationships and lays the groundwork for new ones to enrich life with diverse perspectives and shared humanity.

6.2 Conflict Resolution Strategies for Peaceful Outcomes

Picture this: you're in the middle of a heated debate with a friend with raised voices and emotions running high. We've all felt the tension that happens when disagreements escalate.

Conflict resolution can pave the way to peaceful outcomes. Compromise happens when each party yields something to reach an acceptable solution. This is like meeting in the middle to settle a dispute. Compromise is effective for quick resolutions but may not fully satisfy either side.

On the other hand, **collaboration** seeks a win-win outcome where both parties work together to find solutions that satisfy everyone's needs. Doing so strengthens relationships but requires time and effort. There is also avoidance, where one side withdraws from the conflict, which may provide temporary relief but leave basic issues unresolved.

Accommodation is the cousin of compromise, where parties agree to satisfy certain needs to achieve harmony. While it can diffuse immediate tension, it may lead to resentment if one party uses it habitually.

Resolving conflict amicably requires structure, starting with core issues. Surface arguments can mask deeper problems, so dig deep enough to understand the true causes of disagreement and start brainstorming solutions together.

- Collaborative efforts encourage creativity where all perspectives are considered.
- List potential solutions without judgment and evaluate them to determine the most viable option.
- Implement agreed-upon actions to clearly define roles and responsibilities so everyone knows what's expected.
- Follow up to monitor progress and adjust as needed. A structure can resolve conflict and build trust and cooperation.

Staying calm during conflict prevents escalation. It's easy to get swept up in emotions, but maintaining composure can lead to more productive outcomes.

- Deep breathing exercises are effective techniques for managing emotions. When tensions rise, inhale deeply through your nose, hold for a few seconds, and then exhale slowly through your mouth. This simple act helps center

thoughts and reduce stress. If emotions stay high, it might be necessary to take a timeout.
- Stepping away allows both parties to cool down and regain perspective. Use timeouts to review your feelings and consider the other person's viewpoint. Then, return to the discussion with a clear mind to continue constructive conversation.

Sometimes, conflicts require *mediation* from a third party. When both parties fail to reach a resolution, seek help from a mutual friend or counselor for a neutral perspective.

- Mediators facilitate communication, helping everyone to express concerns without interruption.
- Mediators guide discussions to keep them focused on finding solutions instead of placing blame.
- External support can be invaluable, especially when emotions cloud judgment.
- Choose a mediator both parties trust and respect to assist, but not dictate, the outcome.
- Mediation resolves conflict and equips you with skills to handle future disagreements effectively.

6.3 Maintaining Healthy Boundaries with Friends and Family

Picture your family gathering surrounded by laughter and conversation. However, you feel a twinge of discomfort when a relative asks deeply personal questions. This is where boundaries come in.

Boundaries are invisible lines that protect well-being and help preserve healthy relationships.

- Personal boundaries define behaviors that are acceptable and those that aren't, ensuring respectful interaction grounded in mutual understanding.
- Emotional boundaries safeguard your feelings to protect you from unwanted intrusion by others. Boundaries help you manage your emotions without being overwhelmed by the emotions of those around you.
- On the other hand, physical boundaries protect your personal space and physical touch, prioritizing your comfort and safety in any interaction.

Communicating and enforcing boundaries can be challenging, but they are crucial skills that maintain healthy relationships. Set your boundaries calmly and clearly.

- Choose a neutral moment to express your needs with straightforward language without room for misinterpretation. For instance, if a friend frequently drops by unannounced, you might say, *"I appreciate your visits, but I need a heads-up in advance."* Doing so sets expectations while maintaining respect.
- When boundaries are crossed, address the violation promptly, stating your boundary clearly and explaining why it's important. You might say, *"I was uncomfortable when you shared personal details without asking me first. I choose to keep those matters private."*

Cultural and familial expectations can add complexity to boundary-setting. Different backgrounds can influence how boundaries are perceived and respected. Navigating family obligations, for instance, might require balancing traditional expectations with your personal needs.

In some cultures, family gatherings occur frequently, and participation is expected. While honoring these traditions, it's important to carve out time for yourself so your well-being isn't overshadowed by obligations. Preserving cultural norms while asserting personal needs requires open dialogue. Sharing your perspective with family, along with compromise, can maintain harmony without sacrificing your comfort.

Unhealthy boundaries need to be strengthened for well-being. If you often feel overwhelmed or resentful in certain relationships, your boundaries are being disregarded. Lack of personal space, whether physical or emotional, can lead to feeling suffocated. You might be triggered by constant phone calls, unsolicited advice, or uninvited visits. When those signs appear, it's time to reevaluate your boundaries and make necessary adjustments. You might need to renegotiate the terms of a relationship or reinforce limits with more assertive communication. Maintaining healthy boundaries isn't intended to shut people out; instead, it creates an environment where both parties feel respected and valued.

Scenario	What to Say	How to Respond
Setting a Boundary	"I appreciate your help, but I need to handle this on my own right now."	"Thank you for understanding. I'll reach out if I need assistance."
Declining a Request	"I can't commit to that right now, but I'd be happy to help another time."	"I understand. Let me know when you're available."
Addressing a Misunderstanding	"I think we might have different perspectives on this. Can we talk it through to clarify?"	"I see your point. Let's work together to find a solution."

Acknowledging Someone's Efforts	"I noticed the effort you put into this project—it really made a difference."	"Thank you for saying that. I'm glad it was helpful."
Responding to Feedback (Positive or Negative)	"I appreciate your feedback. I'll think about how I can use this to improve."	"Thanks for being open to the feedback—it's clear you want to grow."
Expressing a Concern	"I felt uncomfortable when [specific action] happened. I'd like us to find a way to avoid that in future."	"I'm sorry you felt that way. Let's figure out a solution together."
Offering Support	"I'm here if you want to talk or need help with anything."	"I appreciate that. I might take you up on it later."

6.4 Roommate Dynamics

Living with roommates is a rite of passage for many young adults, featuring both camaraderie and challenges. The key to harmonious coexistence is establishing *clear expectations from the get-go*.

- It's critical to set ground rules that prevent misunderstandings and conflicts. You might draft a roommate agreement to start. It doesn't have to be formal; it can be a simple list that outlines shared responsibilities and personal boundaries.
- Don't forget to discuss chores! Decide who takes out the trash, who cleans the kitchen, and how often those tasks should be completed. Transparency sets the tone for mutual respect and responsibility, so everyone knows their role in maintaining shared space.

Communication is the lifeline for any successful roommate relationship. It's not enough to set rules and hope they stick; ongoing dialogue is necessary to address issues that arise.

- Regular check-in meetings can be valuable as opportunities to touch base, discuss concerns, and celebrate what's working.
- Shared calendars or apps keep everyone in the loop about schedules and commitments.
- Digital coordination avoids conflicts such as double-booking the living room for study sessions or social gatherings.

Keeping communication open and honest builds trust and supports a living environment where everyone feels valued and heard.

Despite the best-laid plans, **conflicts** are bound to happen. The trick is to handle them with grace and understanding. Negotiating shared spaces and privacy requires empathy.

If a roommate needs quiet time, respect their space just as you want yours to be respected. Addressing noise or cleanliness concerns requires tact. Approach the topic by expressing how the situation affects you by saying, "*When the music is loud, it's hard for me to concentrate.*" You communicate your needs and invite collaboration to reach a solution.

Remember that compromise is necessary in many situations, where common ground can lead to increased harmonious home life.

Creating a ***positive living environment*** benefits everyone. A harmonious home contributes to well-being by providing a refuge from daily life stress. Imagine coming home after a long day to a space that feels welcoming and supportive. That sense of peace and stability is invaluable, affecting your mood, your productivity, and relationships outside the home.

Cultivating such an environment requires effort from all parties. This includes being considerate of each other's needs, celebrating milestones together, and supporting each other during challenges. When everyone contributes to a positive atmosphere, your home becomes a sanctuary where each roommate thrives.

6.5 Romantic Relationships in the Digital Age

When you're *texting* someone you like, and as you wait for their response, you feel a small thrill. Technology has reshaped how we form and maintain romantic relationships, making communication instant and constant. Texting with emoji shorthand has become the primary language of love for many young adults. It's convenient but open to misinterpretation. A message without tone can easily be misconstrued, leading to misunderstandings or anxiety.

Social media adds another layer where your relationship is on display to the whole digital world. It can be challenging to share moments online without letting it dictate the course of your relationship.

Healthy digital communication is key to maintaining respect and understanding.

- Set phone boundaries when you're trying to have quality time together. Agree on times when phones are put away so both of you are fully present. This small step can significantly enhance your connection with each other. Recognize that online miscommunications are common.
- Texts lack the nuance of voice and facial expressions, so when in doubt, pick up the phone or meet in person to clarify intent. Trust and transparency are the bedrock of digital interactions.

- Together, discuss privacy about sharing passwords or maintaining individual space. Some couples exchange passwords as a gesture of trust, while others prefer keeping boundaries. The key is open dialogue so both partners feel comfortable and respected.

Dating apps present their own set of challenges and opportunities. They offer a vast pool of potential matches but can also lead to superficial connections. Genuine relationships focus on authenticity rather than crafting a perfect profile.

- Be upfront about your intentions and interests from the start. Honesty sets the tone for meaningful conversations and connections. However, be mindful of red flags, like inconsistent communication or reluctance to meet in person, which can indicate a lack of sincerity.
- Take your time getting to know someone, moving conversations from an app to real-life interaction when you're ready. Building trust and understanding offline solidifies the foundation of digital communication, transforming potential matches into real partners.

In today's world, managing the digital landscape of love and romance requires a blend of modern mastery and timeless wisdom. Balancing the convenience of technology with the intimacy of personal interaction can enrich relationships, making them more fulfilling and resilient.

Scenario	What to Say	How to Respond
Setting Phone Boundaries During Quality Time	"Let's agree to put our phones away during dinner so we can focus on each other."	"That sounds good. I'd like us to be more present during our time together."
Addressing Miscommunication Online	"I feel like my message may have come across differently than I intended. Can we talk in person or over the phone?"	"I appreciate you clarifying. Let's talk—it's easier to understand each other that way."
Discussing Privacy in Digital Habits	"I value transparency, but I also think it's important we maintain some individual space. What do you think?"	"I agree. Let's find a balance that works for both of us."
Sharing Intentions on Dating Apps	"I'm looking for a meaningful relationship, and I want to be upfront about that. What are you looking for?"	"I appreciate your honesty. I'm looking for something similar, so I'm glad we're on the same page."
Handling Red Flags in Digital Communication	"I've noticed our conversations rarely move beyond the app. Are you interested in meeting in person sometime?"	"Thanks for bringing that up. Let's plan a time to meet—I'd like to get to know you better offline."
Recognizing Superficial Connections	"I want to focus on meaningful conversations rather than just surface-level chats. What do you enjoy talking about?"	"I appreciate that. Let's talk about something deeper—I love discussing [insert topic]."

6.6 Building a Supportive Social Network

You're going through a tough exam season, your stress level is high, and it feels like you're carrying the weight of the world on your shoulders. You could really use a friend to talk to! A strong social support system can be your lifeline in such situations. Friends and family provide emotional support, helping you weather challenges with advice, empathy, and a listening ear. They're the ones who celebrate your successes and offer comfort during setbacks, making life's high points higher and the low points more bearable.

A supportive network also encourages personal growth by pushing you to pursue new opportunities and offering constructive feedback.

Those relationships enrich your life with a sense of belonging and shared experiences that enhance your life and well-being.

Expanding your social circle can be daunting at times, but it's a valuable endeavor. Consider joining clubs or interest groups about your hobbies or passions. Book clubs, sports, or a creative writing group are natural opportunities to meet like-minded individuals and form lasting friendships.

Volunteering in community activities is an excellent way to broaden your network. Not only do you contribute to a cause you care about, but you also meet people who share similar values. These environments foster camaraderie and collaboration, laying the groundwork for meaningful friendships that may last a lifetime.

In any healthy friendship, ***reciprocity*** is fundamental. Relationships thrive on mutual support and give-and-take. Being there for friends in times of need shows you value and respect the relationship. It's not just about offering help but also accepting it. Exchanging support strengthens bonds by building trust and loyalty over time. When both parties invest in a relationship, it grows into a robust support system that can weather any storm. Remember, friendships are about standing by each other through thick and thin.

In the technology age, social media has transformed how friendships are formed and maintained. Digital connections complement real-life relationships by offering convenient ways to stay in touch. However, they can also blur boundaries that, at times, hinder genuine interaction. Learning to balance online and offline interactions is crucial. While it's easy to send a quick message or like a post, they shouldn't replace face-to-face communication. Aim for a healthy mix of digital and personal interactions. Use social media to enhance your connections, but prioritize having quality time together in person. Those real-world experiences deepen friendships and shared memories that a screen can never replicate.

As you reflect on building relationships, remember that building a network of supportive connections is an ongoing process of new experiences of offering support and balancing the digital with what's real. These relationships provide foundations of stability and support to enrich your life with diverse perspectives and shared moments. With these connections, you're better equipped to navigate the challenges of young adulthood, where you're never truly alone. As we move forward, next, we'll explore how these skills apply to moving into and through college life.

Share Your Thoughts, Help Others Grow

If you've enjoyed the book so far, please share your thoughts to help others who are just starting out on their journey and show them they're not alone in their struggles.

How Your Review Helps:

- ***Support another student*** in overcoming everyday hurdles.
- ***Encourage peers*** to pursue their dreams with confidence.
- ***Empower others*** to balance work, school, and social life.

Leaving a review is quick and free, but it can profoundly impact another young adult's life.

Ready to Help?

Scan the QR code below to share your experience. Your insights can inspire and uplift others.

Thanks for helping make a difference!

7

Navigating College Life

"Education is not preparation for life; education is life itself."

John Dewey

Standing in your dorm room surrounded by boxes, you may suddenly realize that this is where you'll forge independence and create a home away from home filled with an exciting future in your new college life. Housing is your sanctuary, your study spot, and a social hub all rolled into one. Choosing the right housing at college requires careful consideration of multiple factors. Look for proximity to campus and amenities for easy access to classes, libraries, and social spots without a long commute. Cost and affordability play a significant role in determining where to live— a bustling campus dorm or a cozy off-campus apartment. Safety is paramount, so research local crime rates and building security features so you have peace of mind. Also, check out study spaces and facilities, like student lounges or group study rooms, which are conducive to quiet learning.

7.1 Choosing the Right Housing

Deciding between on-campus and off-campus housing has pros and cons, just like many things in life. **On-campus dorms** offer a community vibe with social opportunities and events to easily meet people and get involved. When you live in a dorm, you're steps away from classes and campus resources, and it's a lifesaver when you have early-morning lectures or late-night study sessions. But dorm life often comes with limited privacy and cramped spaces.

In contrast, **off-campus apartments** give you a taste of independence and privacy, where you can create a personal space tailored to your preferences. You can choose your roommates and set your own rules. However, off-campus living requires more responsibility like managing bills or commuting to class, where social networks are more spread out.

Deciding on housing options can be complicated, but there are strategies to simplify things.

- Start your search early and use online platforms to explore available options such as price and amenities such as laundry facilities to narrow down choices.
- Attend housing fairs hosted by your university to meet landlords and learn what's available. Networking with peers can yield valuable leads or roommate possibilities.
- When you find a place you're interested in, read the lease agreement carefully. Understand terms like lease duration, security deposits, and pet policies if you plan to bring a furry friend. Diligence can prevent unpleasant surprises,

and you must know your full commitment before signing on the dotted line.

Living with roommates and dealing with landlords can present challenges, but they're not insurmountable. Clear communication is key to managing disputes, noise, or shared expenses. Set ground rules from the start and hold regular check-ins to address issues before they escalate. If conflicts arise with landlords, such as delays in maintenance, document communication right away and know your rights as a tenant. Being proactive and informed can help you manage those situations confidently for a pleasant living experience. If maintenance issues persist, consider reaching out to university housing resources for guidance or mediation. Address challenges quickly, and don't hesitate to communicate for the best experience that supports your personal satisfaction and academic success.

Reflection Section

When you consider your housing needs and preferences, *are you more inclined toward dorm life, or do you prefer the independence of off-campus living?* Decide what matters most to you, like proximity to campus, cost, or social opportunities and personal space. Know your priorities and use them to guide your housing search so your new home meets your academic and personal goals.

- *Do I prefer a vibrant community or more independence?*

- *How important is proximity to campus for me?*

....

- *What is my budget for housing?*

....

- *What balance do I want between social opportunities and personal space?*

....

- *What are my top priorities in a living arrangement?*

....

- *How does this choice support my academic and personal goals?*

....

7.2 Effective Study Techniques

It's easy to feel overwhelmed by the sheer volume of material you need to study before your next big exam. This is common, and you need to know how you learn best because everyone learns differently. Knowing your personal *learning style* can significantly enhance your academic performance.

- Visual learners excel with information presented via charts, diagrams, or color-coded notes. Drawing mind maps with vivid imagery or using flashcards helps them cement concepts.
- If you're an auditory learner, you might benefit from listening to lectures or joining discussion groups. Recording your notes and playing them back or teaching a friend can reinforce your understanding.
- Kinesthetic learners, on the other hand, thrive with hands-on activities. They might find role-playing or using physical objects to demonstrate concepts helps them grasp complex ideas.

Improving *concentration and retention* during study sessions often hinge on the strategies you employ. Active reading is a valuable method to engage with the text as you read. Highlight key points, jot down questions, and summarize sections in your own words to keep you focused for your best comprehension. Note-taking is an essential skill. Consider using the **Cornell method**, where you divide your page into sections for notes, cues, and summaries. This format encourages capturing important details to review them later. Mnemonic devices are particularly useful for memorizing lists or complex information. Creating acronyms or rhymes can transform dry facts into memorable chunks, making it easier to recall them during exams.

Your *study environment* is key to your academic success. A clutter-free study area enhances focus since a tidy space can lead to a clear mind. Arrange your materials for easy access to eliminate distractions like clutter or extraneous gadgets. Some students find that a quiet environment is best for concentration, while others prefer ambient noise or music. If you're the latter, you might want to try listening to background music designed for studying in a comfortable atmosphere to maintain focus. Experiment with different environments to discover what works best for you—a silent library or the hum of a coffee shop.

Campus resources are invaluable for academic support, yet many students overlook them. Tutoring centers offer personalized help in subjects you find challenging, providing insights and explanations that make a big difference. These centers often employ peer tutors who have taken the same courses and understand the material from a student's perspective. Study groups and workshops are also excellent avenues for collaborative learning. Engaging with peers allows you to see different viewpoints, ask questions, and increase your understanding of the subject. Workshops often cover a range of topics, from study skills to exam preparation for maximum academic success.

Navigating college academics requires more than just putting in the hours. Knowing yourself as a learner and creating a good study environment fosters growth. When you embrace your learning style, use effective study techniques, and leverage resources around you, you can transform your study approach. A proactive mindset can improve your grades and enhance your college experience by equipping you with skills to use throughout life.

7.3 Balancing Work and Study

You wake up yawning to another busy day, knowing you have classes to attend, assignments to complete, and working a shift at your part-time job. Balancing work and academics can seem like a juggling act, but managing both responsibilities can lead to immense personal and professional growth through time management.

Prioritizing tasks lets you develop skills you'll have throughout your life. It teaches you how to assess needs from large to small and what can wait so your job and studies never suffer. Juggling multiple commitments makes you more adaptable and prepared for the demands of the business world.

Gaining work experience in college has benefits beyond a paycheck. This is your chance to apply classroom learning to real-world settings in tandem with academic pursuits. For instance, working in a field related to your major can enhance your understanding of theoretical concepts. It's also an opportunity to start building a professional network. The connections you make at your part-time job can lead to references and recommendations that are valuable assets when you apply for full-time positions after graduation. Additionally, the practical skills you learn on the job are transferable and enhance your resume.

Scheduling is key to effectively managing dual roles. A digital calendar can help you organize daily and weekly responsibilities to help you visualize commitments. Set boundaries for work and study time by dedicating specific hours for schoolwork and times you're available to work. Discuss your academic commitments with your employer and negotiate flexible work hours during exams. Most supervisors understand the demands of student life, and they're willing to accommodate reasonable requests to help you thrive academically and professionally.

Part-time work in college is a chance to explore different career paths and develop skills that serve you in the future. Every job teaches valuable lessons where you learn how to manage time, work in a team, and handle responsibilities—all skills that employers value. Moreover, the experience of balancing work and academics can build resilience to prepare you for the challenges of a full-time career. Your resilience, coupled with prioritizing and managing tasks, will make you a more competitive candidate in the job market.

When ***discussing your needs with your employer,*** approach the conversation with clarity and confidence. Explain your academic schedule and the importance of flexibility during times like finals week. Most employers appreciate honesty and are willing to work with you to find a solution that benefits both parties. Seek understanding and ways to accommodate your responsibilities, such as swapping shifts with coworkers or working extra hours during slow periods. A proactive approach not only helps you maintain a healthy balance but also demonstrates your commitment and responsibility, traits that will serve you well in any professional setting.

7.4 Engaging Campus Life

Picture yourself walking across the quad where groups of students discuss their latest club projects or plan the next big event. Engaging in campus life offers rich college experiences with personal and professional benefits. Extracurricular activities serve as platforms to build social connections and friendships for a sense of belonging. You might be interested in a debate club, a sports team, or a cultural society, and these groups introduce you to like-minded peers and expose you to diverse perspectives. These environments foster camaraderie and friendships forged via shared interests and goals.

- Participating in those activities allows exploring interests and discovering passions you might otherwise encounter. You may be captivated by a new hobby or uncover a hidden talent. Exploration can ignite a passion that shapes

your future career or a valued personal pursuit for giving a deeper understanding of yourself and your capabilities.
- Getting involved and making new friends is often as rewarding as the activities themselves, with opportunities to step out of your comfort zone and grow.
- Finding the right activities for you is a process of exploration. Look for clubs, fairs, or interest meetings to learn about different organizations and meet current members. These events are designed to showcase what each group offers by explaining their activities and culture. It's also helpful to research student organizations online. Most campuses have directories or social media pages where groups share information about their missions and upcoming events. Research can help you narrow your options to help you choose activities that resonate with your personal and professional goals.

Balancing involvement with academics makes the most of your college experience. While it's tempting to join every club that interests you, set realistic limits to prevent burnout. Prioritize activities that offer personal growth, leadership opportunities, or skill development. Make sure your academic load allows enough time for your studies and extracurriculars. Balance allows full engagement with each commitment to enrich your college experience without compromising your academic performance.

Campus involvement is a strategic way to enhance your resume and open post-graduation doors. Participation in clubs and organizations shows your initiative, teamwork, and leadership skills, all qualities employers value.

- Organizing events, managing budgets, or leading a project are tangible examples of your abilities. Highlight them on your resume, explaining the contributions and skills you've developed. Additionally, campus activities can lead to valuable networking opportunities. The connections you make with peers, faculty, and guest speakers can all offer insights, mentorship, and potential job leads.

Engaging in campus life is a foundation for personal development and future success. The skills and relationships you build through extracurricular activities will serve you well long after graduation and will enrich your personal and professional lives throughout life. As you move through your college years, remember that these experiences are formative, shaping your goals and skills and the path you take beyond them.

8

Crafting Your Career Path

"The only way to do great work is to love what you do."

Steve Jobs

Picture yourself at a bustling career fair in a room buzzing with energy and opportunity where employers are eager to meet potential candidates. You're assessing a sea of booths as potential gateways to your future, where networking is a valuable skill for connecting and collaborating. Look for professional networks that open doors to job referrals, mentorship, and industries you might otherwise never reach. Networking is a key part of building relationships that grow, evolve, and lead to successful careers.

8.1 Building Professional Networks from Scratch

Networking is critical to future success. It's a bridge to career opportunities and platforms to gain valuable insights from industry veterans. Well-placed connections can lead to firsthand knowledge that moves you forward. Networking is an excellent source of job referrals that increase your chances of finding the right position. Moreover, don't overlook mentorship opportunities to learn from those who are already established on the career path you seek. Mentors provide guidance, share experiences, and offer advice to help you handle challenges and find opportunities that showcase your skills.

Building and maintaining ***professional relationships*** requires effort and strategy. A good start is attending industry events to meet professionals in your field. Conferences, workshops, and seminars are great places to make connections, converse with potential colleagues, exchange ideas, and establish relationships with people who share your interests. Professional associations are excellent networking opportunities. These organizations offer networking events, resources, and forums to connect with peers and experts. Membership in associations expands your contacts and keeps you informed about industry trends and developments.

The digital age has revolutionized networking with tools that help you gain skills and build expertise. **LinkedIn** is a powerful platform for professional networking. Build a solid LinkedIn profile that accurately shows your skills, experiences, and aspirations. A well-crafted profile is a digital resume showcasing your professional identity to potential employers, colleagues, and connections. Look for relevant online forums where you can participate in discussions and share insights. Such interactions expand your network and establish a presence as a knowledgeable, seasoned professional.

Networking yields benefits and access to professional relationships, opportunities, and contributions you can make to your industry. Helping others builds goodwill and trust. These gestures strengthen your network and standing in your profession. Follow up with every new contact, stay in touch, and continue to offer value. The relationships you build are dynamic; they evolve as you and your contacts build your careers.

Interactive Exercise: Networking Action Plan

- Create a networking action plan to guide future efforts.
- Identify three industry events or associations you want to be part of and set specific goals for each.
- Decide who you want to connect with and what you want to learn.
- Optimize your LinkedIn profile, focusing on skills and achievements that fit your career goals. Set a goal to attend one online forum discussion per week.
- This plan can open networking opportunities to help you build a network that enhances your career aspirations and growth.

Networking Goal	Steps to Achieve It	Target Outcome
1. Attend Industry Events or Join Associations	List 3 events or associations and goals for each (e.g., meet 5 new people, learn about trends).	Describe what you aim to gain from these engagements (e.g., build connections, gain insights).
2. Optimize LinkedIn Profile	Outline steps to improve your profile (e.g., update skills, add a professional headshot).	Explain how these updates will help align your profile with career goals.
3. Engage in Online Discussions	Plan to participate in 1 forum discussion per week. List topics or communities of interest.	Describe what you hope to achieve (e.g., visibility, knowledge exchange).

8.2 Crafting a Standout Resume and Cover Letter

Writing a *resume* is like composing your personal story and achievements so that employers will read to understand who you are and what you bring to the table.

- Start with your contact information: your name, phone number, and email address. Make sure the information is up-to-date and professional.
- Next, insert a professional summary of your career to date, highlighting key achievements and your career aspirations. This section should be concise and impactful so the reader has a clear picture of your career to date.
- Next, show your work experience and achievements, listing your positions in reverse chronological order and focusing on work that shows your growth and accomplishments. Use bullet points to detail your responsibilities and highlight specific achievements detailing the impact of your achievements. List skills and certifications next, including each achievement and competency. Tailor the list of the job you're applying for, featuring your most relevant skills front and center.

You'll be competing with a sea of other job seekers, so making your resume stand out can be a tall order. Start by carefully tailoring your job description and looking for keywords and phrases that appear frequently. These are the skills and experiences employers value most. Use your keywords enough to show that you understand the job description and its requirements. Highlight relevant experiences that demonstrate your ability to perform the core responsibilities.

If you manage a team and the job emphasizes leadership, make sure your skills and experience are prominently featured. Customizing a resume shows the employer that you understand their needs and that you have the skills and background to handle them.

A *cover letter* is your opportunity to speak directly to the hiring manager, show your interest in the company and how your skills fit the job requirements. Your letter should address the hiring manager by name, a personal touch that helps set the right tone. In the opening paragraph, express genuine interest in the company and the role you'll play. This is where you express your interest in the company's mission and values, showing that you're qualified and also a good cultural fit.

In the body of the letter, provide specific examples of how your skills and experiences make you an ideal candidate. Use a narrative style to highlight key achievements, drawing parallels between past successes and the challenges or goals of the position. This approach shows you've done your homework and understand how you can contribute to the company's success.

Common pitfalls in resumes and cover letters can undermine your efforts, so it's important to be vigilant.

- Avoid overly generic language that misses the specific qualities that make you a unique candidate.
- Phrases like hard-working or team player are clichés that can make your application fade into the background. Instead, focus on concrete examples and action verbs that convey your contributions and achievements.
- Typos and formatting errors can be bombs that detract from your professionalism.
- Proofread your documents meticulously or ask a trusted friend to review them.
- Formatting such as uniform font size and spacing makes your resume and cover letter easy to read and visually appealing.
- Attention to those details reflects a commitment to quality and thoroughness that impresses a positive impression that potential employers will remember.

8.3 Mastering the Art of the Job Interview

You're sitting in a waiting room, nerves tingling as you prepare to meet a potential employer. The job interview is a pivotal moment in the job search process, and understanding its various formats can help you tailor your preparation.

One common format is the ***behavioral interview,*** where employers assess how you've handled situations in the past to predict future performance. Questions might cover how you've managed team conflict or met a challenging deadline. This interview style requires reflection on experiences and the ability to articulate them clearly.

There's also the ***technical interview,*** often used in fields like engineering or IT, where you're asked to solve problems or demonstrate specific skills related to the job. This type demands a strong grasp of technical knowledge and the ability to apply it under pressure.

Panel interviews, on the other hand, involve multiple interviewers from different departments. They assess your fit from various perspectives, requiring you to engage with each panelist and address diverse concerns.

Preparation is key to being confident and ready for any interview. Start by researching the company and the role you're applying for. Be sure you understand its mission, values, and recent achievements. That knowledge will help you tailor your answers and convey genuine interest in the company.

Practice common interview questions, focusing on clear, concise responses. Use the **STAR method: Situation, Task, Action, Result**, to structure your answers.

For instance, if you're asked about a time you faced a challenge, describe the situation, explain the task at hand, outline the actions you took, and conclude with the results. This method ensures your responses are organized and impactful. You should also prepare insightful questions to ask the interviewers. Inquire about team dynamics, company culture, and expectations for the role. Thoughtful questions demonstrate your interest and engagement and assess whether the company is the right fit for you.

Handling difficult questions gracefully is a skill that can make or break an interview.

- When faced with a tricky question, such as addressing a gap in employment or a weakness, remain calm and composed. Take a moment to gather your thoughts before responding.
- Honesty is crucial, so frame your answer positively. If discussing a weakness, mention steps you're taking to improve.

For example, *"I struggled with public speaking, so I enrolled in a course to build confidence."* This approach shows self-awareness and a commitment to growth. Similarly, when asked why you left a previous job, focus on the future rather than past grievances. *"I left to pursue opportunities that more closely match my career goals"* keeps the conversation positive and forward-looking.

The interview doesn't end when you walk out the door.

- Follow up with a thank-you note or email to leave a good impression. In your message, express gratitude for the opportunity to interview and reiterate your enthusiasm for the position.
- Mention specific points from the interview that made an impression and reinforce your fit for the position.

- Additionally, take time to reflect on your interview performance.
- Consider what went well and areas for improvement.
- Reflection is a valuable learning tool, helping you prepare for future interviews with confidence and insight.

Scenario	What to Say	How to Respond
Explaining a Gap in Employment	"I took time off to focus on [specific reason, e.g., skill development, family], and I'm now ready to apply what I've learned."	"Thank you for sharing. It's great to hear you used that time productively."
Discussing a Weakness	"One area I'm working on is [specific weakness]. I've started [specific action, e.g., taking a course] to improve."	"I appreciate your honesty. It's good to see you're proactive about personal development."
Why Did You Leave Your Last Job?	"I left to pursue opportunities more aligned with my career goals and growth in [specific field]."	"That makes sense. It's important to find roles that align with your aspirations."
Handling Overqualification Concerns	"I'm eager to bring my experience to this role and contribute effectively while also learning and growing."	"That's a great perspective. It's good to know you value both contributing and learning."
Responding to Salary Expectations	"Based on my research and experience, I'm looking for a salary in the range of [range]. Could you share more about the budget for this role?"	"Thank you for being upfront. We'll take that into consideration."

8.4 Navigating Workplace Culture: Tips for Success

You've just started a new job where the environment is exciting but also unfamiliar, where each office hums with activity. Workplace culture is the lifeblood of any organization, shaping how you and your colleagues interact, make decisions, and, ultimately, your work satisfaction. Workplace culture encompasses a company's values and mission, which guide goal setting. It also includes a work environment ranging from formal to relaxed and team dynamics that influence collaboration and morale. A positive culture fosters innovation and job satisfaction, while a toxic culture often leads to burnout and disengagement.

Adapting to a new workplace culture requires a keen sense of observation and a willingness to learn. Pay attention to how your colleagues communicate and interact. *Are meetings formal or informal? Do people prefer emails or face-to-face discussions?* Those nuances provide valuable insights into unspoken rules that govern the workplace.

Team-building activities are effective ways to integrate new settings. Casual lunch, a company retreat, or a team project are activities that help connect with coworkers on a personal level to build trust and camaraderie. It's also an opportunity to showcase your strengths and contributions to reinforce your place on the team.

Communication is the backbone of any successful workplace. Effective communication skills are essential for navigating workplace culture and achieving professional success.

Active listening is a key component to truly hear what others are saying by planning your response to transform your interactions. Good listening skills help to create a collaborative atmosphere that includes concise email writing. Emails these days are typically the primary mode of communication in many workplaces. Your ability to convey a message succinctly saves time and reduces misunderstandings. Brevity and clarity should always be your guiding principles.

Office politics can be a minefield, but with the right training and strategies, they can be handled professionally. Building alliances with coworkers is one approach that identifies colleagues with similar goals to support each other with genuine connections based on mutual respect and shared objectives.

- Focusing on work objectives is another way to avoid potential conflicts.
- Keep your eye on the goal and deliver quality work to position yourself as a valuable team member.
- Avoid getting caught up in office drama or conflicts that don't concern you. Instead, channel your energy into your projects with positive, constructive contributions.

As you immerse yourself in your new workplace culture, remember that curiosity and open-mindedness are your best allies. Embrace the diversity of perspectives and experiences around you and be willing to adapt and learn. Each workplace has a blend of people, opportunities, and challenges. Your ability to navigate this landscape will play a significant role in your professional growth and satisfaction.

8.5 Leveraging Digital Platforms for Career Growth

In the rapidly evolving world of work, digital platforms are indispensable tools for career advancement, with a plethora of fresh opportunities for professional development that were unimaginable a few years ago. Online courses and webinars stand at the forefront, providing accessible avenues for learning new skills without a traditional education.

If you're interested in coding, marketing, or project management, platforms like **Coursera** and **Udemy** offer courses taught by industry experts. These platforms allow you to learn at your own pace, fitting education into your personal schedule. Many of these courses offer certification programs to boost your resume and showcase your commitment to continuous learning. The flexibility and variety of online learning make it an attractive option for young professionals seeking a competitive edge.

Virtual networking events have emerged as popular ways to connect with industry leaders and peers around the globe. These events, ranging from webinars to online conferences, offer opportunities to engage with experts to gain insight into industry trends. Virtual events break down geographical barriers and allow you to participate in discussions and Q&A sessions that increase knowledge and visibility in your field. Participating in these events broadens your perspective and opens doors to collaboration and mentorship opportunities. The key is to approach each event with curiosity and willingness to actively engage. Ask questions and share thoughts to position yourself as a proactive professional.

Your online presence is another key element of career growth, where ***personal branding*** plays a significant role in social media. A personal brand message should complement your online profile with your career goals and values. Make sure your posts, interactions, and the content you share reflect the professional image you want to project. Sharing industry-relevant content positions you as a thought leader and keeps your network engaged to build credibility among peers and potential employers. Your online persona should be authentic and showcase a unique voice and perspective to highlight strengths and achievements.

Digital portfolios have transformed how professionals showcase their work. Digital portfolios are dynamic ways to present achievements. They allow multimedia elements such as videos, presentations, and links to projects. A comprehensive display can set you apart in a competitive job market, offering potential employers rich, engaging insight into your capabilities. A well-organized digital portfolio is a narrative of your professional journey, illustrating growth and accomplishments. As you build your portfolio, highlight projects that best represent your skills and match your career aspirations. Keep it updated and ensure that it reflects your latest work to maintain relevance and impact.

As you embrace digital tools, remember that when you find a job, you also build a career that matches your ambitions and values. The digital landscape offers endless possibilities for growth and connection. Engaging these platforms can significantly enhance your career prospects with skills and networks that thrive in today's dynamic world. As we transition to the next chapter, consider how you might integrate digital strategies into your career by leveraging them into opportunities to drive your professional journey into the future.

9

Money Matters

"Do not save what is left after spending; instead spend what is left after saving."

Warren Buffett

Your favorite coffee shop is buzzing with activity, and finding a place to sit is a challenge while you decide if you should treat yourself to an extra-large latte. It seems like a small decision, but it's one of many daily choices that impact your financial health. For young adults, managing money can feel like wandering a maze filled with unexpected twists and turns.

Understanding money basics is crucial for gaining independence and setting the stage for future success. Let's start by exploring personal finance, which is all about managing money to meet your goals for a secure financial future. Money management is more than budgeting; it's making informed decisions in line with your aspirations.

9.1 Understanding Money Basics

Let's dive into the fundamental financial terms you will encounter. First, assets are things of value that you own, like cash, stocks, or even your laptop. Think of assets as the building blocks of a solid financial foundation. On the flip side, liabilities are what you owe: debts, student loans, or credit card balances.

Balancing assets and liabilities is central to financial stability.

- There's also interest: the cost of borrowing money. Interest works for you when you earn interest on savings; it can also be against you when you pay interest on loans.
- Inflation is another important concept: the rising cost of goods and services over time. It means your money's value decreases unless you invest in ways that outpace inflation.
- Finally, diversification: a strategy to spread investments across different areas to reduce risk. When you understand and apply these terms, you can make decisions that support your financial well-being.

Visual Element: A Cheat Sheet of Financial Terms

Create a simple infographic with definitions and examples of key terms. Use visuals to illustrate how assets and liabilities balance, showing interest as a growing line and depicting inflation with a rising arrow. Keep your cheat sheet handy as a quick reference to reinforce your understanding of these concepts.

Term	Definition	Example
Asset	Anything you own that has value or generates income.	A house, stocks, or savings account.
Liability	Something you owe or an obligation that costs money.	A car loan, credit card debt, or mortgage.
Interest	The cost of borrowing money or the return on invested funds, expressed as a percentage.	Earning 5% annual interest on a savings account or paying 10% on a credit card balance.
Inflation	The rate at which prices for goods and services increase over time.	A loaf of bread costing $1 last year now costs $1.10.
Net Worth	The total value of assets minus liabilities.	If you own $100,000 in assets and owe $40,000, your net worth is $60,000.
Compound Interest	Interest calculated on the initial principal and also on the accumulated interest of previous periods.	Investing $1,000 at 5% compound interest grows to $1,276 in 5 years.
Budget	A plan for managing income and expenses over a specific period.	Allocating $500 for rent, $200 for groceries, and $100 for entertainment each month.
Credit Score	A numerical representation of your creditworthiness.	A score of 700 is considered good, while 500 is poor.

9.2 Create a Budget That Works for You

You're planning a road trip with friends, and the group is mapping the route. You would first map out your route, estimate fuel costs, and plan stops along the way. Budgeting is similar: a financial roadmap to guide you toward your goals to ensure you're prepared for whatever life throws at you. Track your income and expenses to start.

Understanding where your money comes from and where it goes provides control. This is like a detective piecing clues together to see the big picture. This helps you set realistic financial goals, such as saving for a laptop, a dream vacation, or big ambitions for the future.

There are different budgeting methods for different personalities and financial situations. If you enjoy detailed planning, zero-based budgeting might suit you well. This method tracks every dollar to balance income with expenses and savings.

For those who prefer simplicity, the **50/30/20** rule is straightforward, where you allocate 50% of your income to needs, 30% to wants, and 20% to savings or debt repayment. This framework offers flexibility while maintaining structure. Understanding these methods empowers you to choose what best fits your lifestyle to make budgeting less daunting and more intuitive.

To help you start, consider a monthly budget planner. This tool organizes your finances by tracking income, expenses, and savings. This is like having a personal assistant to keep things tidy and in check. However, budgeting isn't without challenges. Impulse spending can derail your plans, tempting you to stray from your financial plan. To help, set spending limits and use cash or debit instead of credit. Irregular income can pose a challenge, especially for freelancers or those with fluctuating paychecks. Adjust your budget to accommodate variability by prioritizing essential expenses and savings to maintain stability.

Budgeting Element	Details	Example/Tip
Income	Track all sources of monthly income.	Regular salary, freelance payments, or side hustle earnings.
Fixed Expenses	List essential expenses that remain consistent each month.	Rent, utilities, insurance premiums.
Variable Expenses	Identify expenses that fluctuate month to month.	Groceries, transportation, entertainment.
Savings Goals	Allocate a portion of income toward savings or investments.	Set aside 20% of income for an emergency fund or retirement account.
Spending Limits	Set boundaries for discretionary spending to avoid impulse purchases.	Use cash or a debit card for non-essential expenses instead of credit.
Irregular Income Adjustment	Adjust your budget for fluctuating income by prioritizing essentials and flexible categories.	Base your budget on the lowest expected monthly income and adjust if more income is received.

9.3 Saving for Emergencies and Future Goals

A sudden job loss or unexpected medical bills require an ***emergency fund*** that serves as a safety net. This is a financial cushion to shield you from scrambling to cover costs when unforeseen events occur. Without this fund, you might have to rely on credit cards or loans, which can trap you in a debt cycle. To build this fund, set a target amount like three-to-six months of living expenses. You can automate your savings by directing a portion of your paycheck into a separate account you treat as a non-negotiable expense. This way, your savings grow consistently without constant attention.

Saving for short-term and long-term goals also matters. Short-term savings can include a vacation fund or a new gadget as a small reward to keep you motivated. In contrast, long-term savings focus on milestones like buying a home or saving for retirement. Prioritize those goals by assessing their importance and time frame. Diversify your savings so you're prepared for both immediate happiness and future needs.

Different savings accounts offer different interest rates. ***High-yield savings*** accounts offer better returns than standard accounts, which are ideal for emergency funds. ***Certificates of deposit (CDs)*** provide higher interest rates for fixed terms suitable for medium-term goals. When you understand those options, you can choose the best savings vehicles that fit your financial objectives and risk tolerance.

9.4 Understanding Credit Scores and How to Improve Yours

You're at a point in life where a new apartment or a car loan are likely acquisitions on your horizon. This is when your ***credit score*** becomes your silent spokesperson, influencing your financial possibilities. A credit score is a numerical score of your creditworthiness that affects your ability to secure loans and the interest rates you pay. Think of it as a report card for your financial activity, where higher scores generally lead to more favorable loan terms. Lenders use this score to gauge risk by determining if you're a reliable borrower. A robust credit score can mean the difference between approval and rejection or a high interest rate versus a manageable lower rate.

Many factors contribute to your credit score, each playing a role in the amount of money you can borrow. **Payment history** carries the most weight, accounting for roughly 35% of your score. Consistently paying bills on time positively influences this factor. **Credit utilization** is the amount of credit you use compared to the total limit you have, which is about 30%. Keeping this ratio low is considered responsible credit management. **The length of your credit history**, or how long you've maintained credit accounts, affects about 15% of your score. Longer histories generally indicate stability.

There are a few practical strategies that can help you enhance your credit score. Pay your bills promptly; doing so significantly boosts your score over time. Reducing credit card balances can also improve your credit utilization. If you see errors on your credit report, dispute them immediately. Errors can unnecessarily drag your score down. Ignoring credit management can lead to long-term challenges. A low score makes securing loans difficult, and even if approved, you might face higher interest rates or higher insurance premiums, which add financial strain.

9.5 The Basics of Tax and Tax Filing

Understanding taxes seems mysterious to many, but understanding the basics helps make it manageable.

- Income tax is a percentage of your earnings paid to the government. This tax supports essential services like education and infrastructure.
- Sales tax is a small percentage added to the cost of purchased goods, varying by location. It's applied to everyday items like clothing or electronics, lightly impacting your budget.
- Property tax applies if you own property. Your property tax is based on its value and funds local services such as road maintenance and schools.

Each tax type influences your finances differently, affecting how you plan and allocate your resources.

Filing your taxes, though it may seem daunting, can be straightforward with a step-by-step approach.

- Gather the necessary documents, like W-2 forms or 1099 forms that report your income. These documents are the foundation of your tax return, a snapshot of your earnings.
- Next, familiarize yourself with tax brackets that determine your income tax rate. Understanding where you fall helps you figure out your tax liability.
- Deductions and credits significantly reduce the amount you owe. Deductions shrink taxable income for expenses like student loan interest, while credits lower your tax bill directly, often related to education or energy efficiency.

Common tax mistakes can lead to unwanted stress, but awareness helps you avoid them.

- Misreporting income is a frequent error, often stemming from overlooked documents or misunderstood forms.
- Double-check all sources of income for accuracy. Failing to claim eligible deductions is another pitfall.
- Familiarize yourself with the deductions you qualify for to maximize your return.

When you determine whether to file your taxes yourself or utilize professional help, weigh the pros and cons. Tax preparation software simplifies filing with cost-effective solutions for straightforward situations. However, complex tax scenarios can benefit from professional expertise to ensure compliance and potential savings.

9.6 Tackling Student Loans Strategically

When you enter the world of higher education, along with your aspirations often come student loans, a common reality for many. Understanding the available loans can help you through the financial landscape successfully. Federal loans are provided by the government and often come with benefits like income-driven repayment plans that allow payments based on your earnings, and federal loan forgiveness programs for those in qualifying public-service jobs. These options offer flexibility and potential relief, making them favorable choices for many students. On the other hand, private loans from banks or credit unions might offer competitive rates but often lack federal benefits, making them a stricter commitment.

Managing these loans involves strategic planning.

- Setting up automatic payments ensures timely payments to avoid late fees and gradually improve your credit score.

- Prioritizing high-interest loans can save you money in the long run, reducing the overall cost of borrowing. You can integrate loan repayment with your overall financial strategy.
- Consider how these payments will impact your long-term retirement plans or other long-term goals.
- Saving money and planning for the future is a delicate balance to make sure you meet your current obligations without sacrificing future security.

Numerous resources are available to help you manage your student loans. Online tools and services like student loan calculators and financial planning apps help visualize the impact of different payment plans. These tools guide you in making informed decisions to help with complex financial decisions. Financial advisors specializing in student loans can offer personalized advice by tailoring strategies for your personal financial situation. They have the resources to make the daunting task of loan repayment a manageable aspect of your financial plan, empowering you to focus on achieving your monetary goals with confidence.

9.7 Managing Debt Wisely

Students often juggle several financial commitments, including student loans, a credit card for emergencies, and perhaps even a car loan. Understanding how these debts impact your financial health is critical. Debt can be a double-edged sword. **Good debt**, like student loans or mortgages, can be an investment in your future, while **bad debt**, like high-interest credit cards, can drain resources and lead to financial stress. Interest rates play a significant role in how quickly debt can spiral.

A ***high interest rate*** means more of your money goes toward interest rather than reducing the principal balance, which makes it harder to pay off.

Having a ***debt repayment plan*** is a proactive step toward financial freedom. Two popular methods are the debt snowball and the debt avalanche. The debt snowball calls for paying off the smallest debt first and building momentum as you tackle larger debts. The debt avalanche targets debts with the highest interest rates first to save money on interest over time.

- Consolidating debt into a single lower-interest loan can simplify management and reduce interest costs. Credit counseling services provide guidance to help you create a realistic repayment plan.
- Finding reputable agencies is essential; look for those accredited by the National Foundation for Credit Counseling.
- Working with a financial advisor offers personalized strategies to effectively manage and reduce debt.

You can avoid future debt by living within your means and planning for expenses.

- Establish an emergency fund to prevent reliance on credit in emergencies.
- Regularly review and adjust your budget to stay on track by making conscious choices to prioritize long-term financial well-being instead of short-term gratification.

Repayment Strategy	Description	Benefits	Considerations
Debt Snowball	Focus on paying off the smallest debt first, then apply that payment to the next smallest debt.	Builds motivation by achieving quick wins.	May not save as much on interest compared to other methods.
Debt Avalanche	Focus on paying off debts with the highest interest rates first.	Saves money on interest over time.	Progress may feel slower initially, especially with large debts.
Debt Consolidation	Combine multiple debts into a single lower-interest loan.	Simplifies management and reduces overall interest costs.	Requires a good credit score to secure favorable terms.
Credit Counseling	Work with professionals to create a realistic repayment plan and improve financial literacy.	Access to guidance and support for managing debt.	Ensure the agency is reputable and accredited (e.g., by the National Foundation for Credit Counseling).
Financial Advisor	Develop a personalized strategy for managing and reducing debt effectively.	Tailored advice based on individual financial situations.	May involve costs for advisory services.

9.8 Earning and Negotiating

There are times when a surprise income stream comes into your life to bolster your financial security, like winning the lottery. For young adults, *diversifying income* can be a game-changer. You might pick up a side hustle that matches your passions, like freelancing your design skills or selling crafts online. Not only does extra work provide a financial cushion, but it also allows you to explore interests and build new skills.

Passive income, such as renting a spare room or investing in dividend-yielding stocks, adds a layer of security working for you even when you're not actively engaged. Additional income streams give you peace of mind to handle unexpected expenses or save for future goals.

When it comes to *salary negotiation,* preparation is your best ally. Knowledge of industry standards provides a solid foundation to help you negotiate with confidence. Know your worth by understanding the average salary for your position and experience level. Websites like **Glassdoor** and **PayScale** provide valuable insights. During negotiations, articulate your achievements and how they contribute to the organization by demonstrating your value. Practice makes perfect, so consider role-playing with a friend to refine your pitch. Remember, salary isn't the only negotiable aspect—benefits, work flexibility, and professional development opportunities are typical parts of the package.

Advancing in your career is more than just hard work. Investing in further education through formal degrees or online courses can significantly enhance your skills and marketability. Certifications in your field can open doors to new positions and responsibilities to showcase your commitment to professional growth.

Networking is always a powerful tool, and building connections in your industry can lead to mentorship opportunities, job referrals, and insights about emerging trends. Conferences and professional associations also expand your network to showcase your expertise.

9.9 Investing 101: Building Wealth for the Long Term

As a young adult joining the workforce, the money you earn should work for you, growing and multiplying as you focus on your life goals. The essence of investing is putting your money into assets that appreciate over time with compounding returns.

Compound interest is a powerful force where interest on your investment also earns interest, creating a snowball effect that accelerates wealth accumulation. This means your money isn't just sitting idle; it's actively building more wealth. However, investing has its own set of challenges, primarily the balance between risk and reward. Higher potential returns often accompany higher risks, so understand your risk tolerance to make informed decisions.

Over time, you'll encounter various vehicles that cater to different goals and comfort levels.

- Stocks represent ownership in a company with potential for growth but also volatility. Bonds provide fixed-income, safer options compared to stocks.
- Mutual funds pool money from many investors to buy a diversified portfolio of stocks and bonds by spreading risk.
- Real estate, such as direct property investment or real estate investment trusts (**REITs**), offer tangible assets and potential rental income.
- Exchange-traded funds (**ETFs**) are similar to mutual funds but trade like stocks with flexibility and diversification. Each option presents unique opportunities, allowing you to tailor your portfolio to your financial objectives.

When you start investing in the stock market, you'll want to open a brokerage account, which is a gateway to buying and selling stocks. Your account and many online platforms offer easy access and low fees. As you build your portfolio, investigate diversification strategies to mitigate risk. Diversifying spreads investments across different sectors to reduce the impact of a single asset's poor performance. This is a safety net of sorts, so if one area falters, others stabilize your overall returns.

Retirement accounts, such as **401(k)s** or **IRAs**, are essential for building long-term wealth. Thanks to compound interest, investing early in adulthood gives your investments more time to grow. Your contributions are often tax-advantaged and boost your savings further. Retirement savings should be a priority in your future self for financial security when you're ready to enjoy a comfortable retirement.

Investment Option	Description	Benefits	Considerations
Stocks	Ownership in a company, offering potential for high returns but with volatility.	Potential for significant growth and dividends.	High risk; value can fluctuate significantly in the short term.
Bonds	Fixed-income securities that act as loans to corporations or governments.	Safer than stocks, providing steady income.	Lower returns compared to stocks; affected by interest rate changes.
Mutual Funds	Pooled investments in diversified portfolios of stocks and bonds.	Diversifies risk across multiple assets.	Management fees can reduce returns.
ETFs (Exchange-Traded Funds)	Similar to mutual funds but traded like stocks, offering flexibility and diversification.	Lower fees than mutual funds and easily tradable.	Subject to market fluctuations.
Real Estate	Tangible assets offering potential rental income or appreciation.	Provides steady income and portfolio diversification.	Requires significant capital and can involve management responsibilities.
Retirement Accounts (401(k)s, IRAs)	Tax-advantaged accounts for long-term savings.	Compound interest allows growth over time; tax benefits boost savings.	Early withdrawal penalties; limited investment choices in some plans.

9.10 Avoiding Common Financial Pitfalls

Think twice if you hear about an investment opportunity that promises easy money or a life-changing investment opportunity. Scams and easy money schemes are everywhere, targeting young adults who are often new to managing money. Look out for red flags such as requests for personal information, promises of high returns with little risk, or urgent demands that pressure you to act quickly. Always verify the source. If something sounds too good to be true, it probably is. Protect your financial information and always double-check with trusted sources before you proceed.

Long-term independence requires careful planning to ensure that your expenses are covered by income without your constant presence. This is where the FIRE philosophy is your best friend. **FIRE** stands for **Financial Independence to Retire Early**, which means you save aggressively and invest wisely to reach a point where work is optional. This may sound like a dream, but it requires discipline and a different mindset to control expenses and maximize savings. Plan to invest in a diverse portfolio that fits your risk tolerance. Your ultimate goal is to have the freedom and comfort to choose how you spend your time without worrying about your financial future.

As you plan your retirement, remember that awareness and preparation are your best allies. Stay informed and be proactive to avoid common pitfalls for a future of financial security and independence. These financial tools allow you to handle any challenges that may arise.

10

Cultivating an Entrepreneurial Mindset

"I knew that if I failed, I wouldn't regret it, but I knew the one thing I might regret is not trying."

Jeff Bezos

Most people deal with day-to-day frustrations. Successful entrepreneurs often start with a problem that annoys them and set out to find a solution. This chapter guides you to change everyday challenges into opportunities to shift your mindset to look at problems as possibilities that make life easier.

10.1 Identifying Opportunities: Seeing Problems as Possibilities

Changing how you perceive problems is the first step toward cultivating an entrepreneurial mindset. Instead of viewing obstacles as roadblocks, look at them as opportunities for success and innovation. Many businesses have solved minor inconveniences.

- ***Airbnb*** started because the founders couldn't afford to pay rent and decided to rent air mattresses in their apartments. That solution to a personal problem evolved into a global hospitality platform.

When you adopt this perspective, you can train yourself to recognize potential business ideas from the challenges you encounter. This mindset shift enables proactivity to turn problems into stepping stones and create profitable solutions.

You'll need tools and techniques to identify successful business opportunities. One effective tool is the **SWOT** analysis, which stands for **Strengths**, **Weaknesses**, **Opportunities**, and **Threats**. This method helps you to thoroughly evaluate situations and ideas to identify opportunities that could propel you to success.

Assess internal and external factors to gain insights and leverage your skills and abilities to create solutions. Make a point of analyzing trends in emerging markets to spot shifts and coming innovations that may work for you. Staying ahead of trends helps you position yourself to meet future demands and craft solutions before others beat you to it.

Curiosity and continuous learning are key to the entrepreneurial mindset. Staying informed about industry developments helps you to spot opportunities while perusing industry reports and news keeps you current with change and innovation. Be on the lookout for workshops and seminars that expose you to new ideas and perspectives to expand ideas and inspire creative solutions to your problems. They can help you build a network of like-minded people who offer support and collaboration to identify opportunities and act on them.

Interactive Element: Brainstorming and Creative Thinking Exercise

Set aside brainstorming time to solve a problem you face, then branch out with potential solutions and related ideas. Encourage yourself to think without limits, where your goal is to generate as many ideas as possible, even outlandish ones. Once you've done this, review them with a critical eye to identify the most promising ideas. You might consider forming a brainstorming session with peers, where diverse perspectives and ideas can lead to innovative solutions you wouldn't have considered by yourself. A collaborative approach can yield insights and spark creativity, expanding your ability to discover and develop opportunities.

Step	Action	Your Notes
Define the Central Problem/Challenge	Clearly state the problem or challenge you want to address.	
Generate Potential Solutions	List as many ideas as possible, without worrying about practicality at this stage.	
Create a Mind Map	Organize your ideas visually, branching out from the central problem with related thoughts.	
Review and Evaluate Ideas	Critically assess your mind map to identify the most promising solutions.	
Collaborate with Others	Form a group brainstorming session and gather diverse perspectives.	
Select the Best Ideas	Choose the top ideas to explore further and develop into actionable plans.	

10.2 The Basics of Starting Your Own Business

Starting a business often begins with inspiration, but transforming that idea into reality requires careful planning. Crafting a ***business plan*** is your first step. Think of it as a roadmap to achieve your goal. A solid business plan should outline your business goals, strategies to achieve them, and the structure of your operations. Outline financial projections, marketing plans, and the value your business will offer. Next, you need a business plan, which might seem daunting, but it's essential to keep your vision on track to win potential investors for your project.

Market research is another key step to gathering information about the industry, target audience, and competitors. Knowing the market landscape can identify gaps your business can fill to tailor your offerings to meet customer needs. Utilize surveys, focus groups, and data analysis for insights to shape your business strategy for success. Market research is an ongoing process to monitor shifts and trends so you can adapt and stay competitive.

Funding is essential to your entire plan. Many startups need external financing to get off the ground with multiple avenues to explore. Consider traditional bank loans, venture capital, or crowdfunding platforms like **Kickstarter**. Each option has pros and cons; your choice will depend on your business model and financial needs. Securing funding is more than money; it is building relationships with investors who believe in your vision and are able to provide strategic guidance.

Legal and regulatory considerations are the foundation of any legitimate business. One of your first decisions is choosing a business structure. Whether you opt for a sole proprietorship, an LLC, or a corporation, each has legal and tax implications. Register your business name so your business is recognized legally and protects your brand identity. Don't overlook licensing requirements, either. You might need specific permits to operate in your state or country that require legal advice to make sure no laws or requirements are violated.

Your ***business model*** is the backbone of your enterprise. It outlines how your business makes money to sustain itself over time. Identify your target customers—those who benefit most from your products or services. Understanding your audience dictates your marketing and product offerings to meet specific consumer needs. Establishing pricing strategies is equally important. Your pricing should reflect the competitive value your business provides in your industry. This is a delicate but essential balance for ongoing profitability.

Brand development relies on a strong product identity that customers recognize. Your brand is your logo and your story, along with the experience you provide that keeps your customers satisfied and loyal. Design a memorable, distinctive logo that reflects your business values. Crafting a unique value proposition is a key component that sets your business apart from competitors and explains why customers should choose you. A well-defined brand builds trust and loyalty, turning your customers into long-term advocates.

10.3 Intrapreneurship: Career Innovation

Picture yourself in a bustling office surrounded by activity and constant emails. You're part of a dynamic team, each person contributing their skills to move the company forward. *But what if you could do more?* Intrapreneurship can make a significant impact within your organization, where innovation drives change from within without the need to start your own business. Intrapreneurship can foster a culture of creativity and growth to benefit your company and your personal career development.

Intrapreneurship encourages a ***culture of innovation,*** where employees are encouraged to think outside the box and challenge the status quo. Environments like this are fertile ground for new ideas and fresh concepts to flourish and evolve. When employees feel encouraged to experiment and take calculated risks, they're more invested in their work. A sense of ownership enhances job satisfaction, where individuals see their contributions directly impacting company success. Moreover, it paves the way for career growth with opportunities to lead projects and showcase your skills as an invaluable asset to the organization.

Cultivating an intrapreneurial mindset starts with proactivity by looking around your workplace to identify areas that need improvement. Maybe there's an outdated process that seems inefficient. By suggesting new product ideas or streamlined procedures, you demonstrate initiative and creativity. A proactive approach showcases your problem-solving skills and positions you as a forward-thinker who recognizes and seizes opportunities to add value, even outside your job description. This mindset requires curiosity, creativity, and courage to move beyond your role.

Building support for intrapreneurial initiatives is important, as management and team buy-in can make or break innovative projects. Start with data-driven proposals that clearly outline the benefits and potential returns of your idea. Concrete evidence lends credibility to your suggestions so others can see the value of your proposal. Consider pilot programs with measurable outcomes that allow you to test ideas and gather data to prove that the concept can persuade stakeholders to support your vision. Tangible results foster confidence and support from your colleagues to create more products.

Successful examples of intrapreneurship abound in the business world. Take *3 M's Post-It sticky notes*, for instance. What began as a failed adhesive became a staple, thanks to an employee's innovative thinking. This story highlights how an intrapreneurial spirit can transform setbacks into success. Similarly, **Google's 20% time policy** empowers engineers to dedicate a portion of their workweek to passion projects. This initiative led to the creation of products like **Gmail** and **AdSense**, which underscore the immense value of intrapreneurship. These examples illustrate that with the right support and mindset, you can drive significant change and innovation within your organization.

10.4 Building Resilience in the Face of Failure

Your first project is about to be launched; you are filled with excitement and hope. Then, despite all your efforts, it doesn't work out as planned. This scenario is common in entrepreneurship, where setbacks are inevitable. But failure isn't the end; it's a stepping stone to growth. Consider the stories of well-known entrepreneurs who faced defeat but bounced back stronger. Take **J. K. Rowling**, who faced numerous rejections before Harry Potter captured the world's imagination. Or **Steve Jobs**, who was fired from Apple, the company he co-founded only to return and lead it to unprecedented success. These stories exemplify resilience, transforming failures into opportunities that teach perseverance despite challenges.

Developing resilience starts with *self-reflection*. When things don't go as planned, pause and assess what happened. *What were the contributing factors? What can you learn from this experience?* Reflecting on these questions helps you understand mistakes by turning them into valuable lessons. Setting realistic, flexible goals is another strategy. While ambition is important, setting unattainable goals can set you up for disappointment. Give yourself room to adapt as circumstances shift.

Flexibility allows you to navigate changes without feeling defeated to reinforce the idea that success isn't linear but a series of adjustments and learning curves.

A growth mindset requires resilience, viewing challenges as opportunities for development rather than threats to success. When you receive feedback or criticism, listen carefully. It's easy to take it personally, but they offer insights for improvement. Adapt to changing circumstances as part of this mindset. Business landscapes are dynamic, and accepting change is essential. You might decide to alter your strategy or explore new avenues while adaptability keeps you moving forward. This mindset fosters creativity and innovation when you're not bound by fear of failure but instead motivated by growth potential.

Support networks are invaluable for building resilience. Entrepreneurial support groups and mentorship programs provide communities with a way to share experiences and gain insights. These networks offer emotional and practical support to remind you that you're not alone on your journey. Interact with others who have faced similar challenges and found incredible reassurance. Mentors can offer guidance drawn from their own experiences, providing perspectives to help you conquer obstacles. Mentors serve as sounding boards for your ideas, offering encouragement and constructive feedback. These relationships bolster your resilience and enrich your entrepreneurial path.

Reflection Section

Think about a recent setback you faced. *How did it affect you, and what did you learn from it?*

- Write down the emotions you felt and the lessons you discovered. Consider how you can apply those insights to future challenges.
- Reflection helps solidify your experiences as learning opportunities to reinforce your resilience and readiness to tackle whatever comes next.

- *Describe the setback you faced.*

....

- *How did the setback affect you emotionally?*

....

- *What lessons did you learn from this experience?*

....

- *How can you apply these lessons to future challenges?*

....

- *What strengths did you discover in yourself through this process?*

....

10.5 Networking With an Entrepreneurial Mindset

You're at a local event, surrounded by chatter and clinking glasses. Conversations buzz with potential right where your entrepreneurial journey can take off right away. Networking is more than just exchanging business cards; it's building relationships to propel your ideas forward.

For entrepreneurs, strong networks are crucial. They provide access to resources and opportunities that might remain out of reach otherwise. Whether you seek funding or a business partner with complementary skills, your network can open doors you never knew existed.

Networking can uncover hidden resources. When you connect with investors, you gain funding, invaluable advice, and mentorship. Investors often have years of experience offering insights to manage the complex waters of entrepreneurship. Beyond financial support, your network is ripe with potential collaborators. Finding business partners who share your visions brings various strengths that can make all the difference. Together, you can create synergies to amplify your capabilities by turning a simple idea into a groundbreaking venture.

Building an effective network requires strategy and effort. Conferences and events are places to meet like-minded individuals and industry leaders. These gatherings are fertile ground for exchanging ideas and making connections. Don't shy away from introducing yourself and sharing your passions; you never know who might be interested in your story.

Social media platforms are also powerful tools for professional networking. **LinkedIn**, for instance, allows you to connect with professionals worldwide to participate in discussions, join relevant groups, and learn about industry topics that match your interests. An online presence extends your reach beyond local events to share your insights and learn from others.

Giving is key to networking, where you offer and gain knowledge. Sharing knowledge and resources with your network establishes you as a valuable connection. When you support others' initiatives, you build a reputation for yourself by contributing to the community. Generosity often returns tenfold when those you've helped likely support you in return. This is a cycle of reciprocity that strengthens your network and fosters long-lasting relationships built on trust and mutual respect.

Maintaining relationships is the key to longevity and benefit. You might send a quick email to check in or share an article that might interest them. Don't overlook small gestures that keep you on their radar. Remembering birthdays or congratulating someone on a new job goes a long way toward showing genuine interest. Long-term relationships are about ongoing business and building mutual support communities in your industry.

Networking is an ongoing evolution alongside your career. As you grow, so will your network. Each connection brings new opportunities and challenges for lasting personal and professional development. Your relationships provide a support system to guide you in your entrepreneurial community and enrich your growth and career. In addition to networking, the next chapter will explore how connections can enhance your financial acumen and prepare you to manage complex personal and business finances.

11

Embracing Modern Challenges

"We cannot always build the future for our youth, but we can build our youth for the future."

Franklin D. Roosevelt

P icture yourself at your kitchen table with your laptop open and a steaming mug of coffee nearby. The line between workspace and living area blurs, creating a new frontier in your daily routine. This is the reality of remote work, a shift in traditional job roles that's both exciting and challenging. No longer confined by geographical barriers, you can work from anywhere, whether a corner of your home or the bustling café on the corner.

Flexibility is a game-changer here, allowing you to tailor your work environment to fit your lifestyle, reducing travel time and often increasing productivity. In fact, studies show that people working remotely in the US are 22% more likely to report increased productivity (SOURCE 1). Yet, this new way of working also demands a new approach to work-life boundaries, which are easily blurred when your home becomes your office.

11.1 Navigating Remote Work: Tips to Stay Productive

An effective home office can be a boon in the work-at-home landscape. When you set up your home office, you'll need ergonomic furniture. A comfortable chair and desk allow you to focus on your work without discomfort. Invest in a chair that supports your back and a desk that keeps your computer screen at eye level. This improves your posture and enhances productivity. A quiet environment is equally important. If you're easily sidetracked by household chores or the lure of your favorite show, consider a quiet, designated workspace separated from the rest of your home. Even a small corner with a simple desk and chair can make a big difference. Use noise-canceling headphones to block out ambient noise and set clear boundaries with housemates or family to respect your work hours.

In a remote work setting, communication is the lifeline keeping teams connected and cohesive. Without face-to-face interactions, clear, consistent communication is key. Video conferencing tools like **Zoom** or **Microsoft Teams** bridge the distance, allowing you to engage with colleagues in real time. These platforms offer the chance to connect socially, maintaining the camaraderie that office life naturally provides. Regular check-in meetings are vital to keep everyone on the same page so projects progress smoothly. Those meetings provide opportunities to voice concerns, celebrate achievements, brainstorm solutions, and foster a sense of unity and shared purpose.

Self-motivation and accountability are allies in the remote work world, where supervision is often minimal. Establishing a daily routine can anchor your day to stay focused and productive. Set consistent start-and-end times for your workday, just like a traditional office schedule. Structure helps you manage time and signals your brain when it's time to shift from work mode to relaxation. Utilize productivity tools like **Asana** or **Slack** to organize tasks and communicate with your team. These platforms offer features like task assignments, deadlines, and progress tracking, providing a clear overview of your workload and enhancing collaboration.

Reflection Section

Reflect on your remote work experience so far. Jot down what has worked well and the challenges you continue to face. *How did you adapt your space and routine to support productivity? Could your team improve aspects of communication?*

- Reflection can guide you to make small, impactful changes to your remote work setup.
- Tailor your environment and habits to best suit your needs for ongoing growth and development.
- Remember that flexibility, communication, and self-motivation are your best tools to achieve success.

- *What has been working well in my remote work setup?*

....

- *What challenges do I continue to face?*

....

- *How have I adapted my space to support productivity?*

  ....

- *How have I structured my routine for success?*

  ....

- *What aspects of team communication could improve?*

  ....

- *What small changes can I make to enhance my remote work experience?*

  ....

11.2 Building a Personal Brand in the Digital Age

As you scroll through social media one evening, you pause on a profile that catches your eye. It's vibrant, cohesive, and tells a story that resonates with you. That's personal branding in action. In today's digital landscape, the internet serves as a marketplace and a stage where building a personal brand is crucial. The job market is highly competitive, and standing out can make all the difference. A well-crafted personal brand distinguishes you from other candidates by enhancing career opportunities and showcasing your unique skills, passions, and values that reflect who you are and what you represent so you're memorable in the minds of potential employers.

- To begin building your personal brand, identify a unique value proposition about what sets you apart. Start by reflecting your strengths, passions, what drives you, and what you excel at. These are your brand's building blocks.
- Next, write a personal mission statement that states your professional goals and the values that guide you. This is your compass guiding you with direction and clarity as you progress in your career. Assemble all your talents and skills and weave them into a narrative highlighting your journey and aspirations so others understand and connect with your story.

Brand messaging requires consistency. Just as you wouldn't expect a brand like **Apple** to suddenly start using neon colors and Comic Sans, your personal brand should maintain a cohesive look and feel across all platforms.

- Develop a consistent visual and verbal identity that fits your personal values. This includes everything from the photos you choose to the tone of your writing.
- Your online presence should reflect your authentic self with those who share your values and interests.
- Alignment with your peers builds trust and credibility, which are essential components of a strong personal brand.

Leveraging social media is a powerful strategy to expand your brand's reach and influence. Create a professional LinkedIn profile and a digital resume that showcases your achievements and helps you connect with industry professionals.

- Make sure your profile picture is professional, your headline compelling, and your summary tells your unique story.
- Feature content relevant to your field, like sharing articles, commenting on posts, or publishing insights and ideas. These things increase your visibility and position you as a thought leader in your area of expertise.

Twitter is also an effective tool for personal branding. It allows you to engage with industry-related content, join conversations, and network with professionals worldwide. Follow thought leaders and engage with their content by retweeting and adding your perspective. This helps you stay informed about trends and amplifies your voice in digital space. Remember, the goal is to interact and build relationships that may lead to opportunities. Embrace digital tools and platforms to craft a personal brand that is authentic and impactful.

11.3 Digital Etiquette: Managing Your Online Presence

A digital footprint is like a tattoo that follows you across the internet, shaping how others perceive you personally and professionally. This is an invisible trail playing a significant role in your life, especially when potential employers dig deeper into your background. Recruiters often check social media as part of their hiring process, looking for red flags but also glimpses of your character and values.

You just applied for your dream job, knowing that your online presence reflects the best version of yourself as a testament to your professionalism and integrity.

Conversely, a questionable post or an inappropriate photo could raise doubts about your suitability, influencing decisions before you ever step into an interview room. Digital interactions can affect personal relationships. Friends, family, and even potential partners may form opinions based on what you share online, highlighting the importance of managing your digital persona carefully.

Digital etiquette is your guide to navigating the vast online world responsibly and respectfully. At its core, it is interacting in a way that reflects you in a positive light and avoiding harmful or inflammatory comments that can escalate into conflicts or tarnish your reputation. Before posting, consider whether your words make a positive contribution or if they're likely to cause harm or misunderstanding.

Additionally, be mindful of your privacy settings. Social media platforms frequently update their privacy policies, sometimes altering who can see your content. Regular review of those settings ensures that you share information intentionally, not broadcasting it to the world inadvertently. Control who sees your digital self and make sure it matches your real-world values, thoughts, and behaviors. This is a proactive approach to protect your image and maintain a consistent, positive presence across platforms.

In a constantly connected world, digital detoxes offer much-needed respite. Taking breaks from social media and digital devices can significantly reduce screen-induced stress that creeps into life. Constant notifications, updates, and messages create a challenging sense of urgency to truly disconnect and relax. Step away, even temporarily, and let your mind reset to appreciate the present without digital distraction. Breaks encourage in-person interactions, fostering better connections beyond likes and emojis. See yourself having dinner with friends where everyone is fully present, sharing stories and laughter without any interruption of phones buzzing on the table. These moments remind us of the richness of face-to-face communication and the value of being truly engaged with those around you.

In the digital age, literacy extends beyond reading and writing to include understanding and utilizing the online world. Digital literacy helps you connect safely with online interactions.

- Be aware of fake news and misinformation that spreads rapidly across the internet. With so much information at your fingertips, distinguishing fact from fiction requires critical thinking and a skeptical eye.
- Protecting your personal data online is another key component. Cybersecurity threats, from phishing scams to identity theft, require vigilance.
- Use strong, unique passwords for your accounts and enable two-factor authentication whenever possible. This added security layer helps safeguard your information from unauthorized access.
- Staying informed about digital trends and security measures equips you to interact online with confidence, so your digital footprint remains positive, and your personal data is protected.

11.4 Understanding and Embracing Diversity and Inclusion

Many workplaces these days are familiar with diversity and inclusion. These are recognized concepts where every voice matters, and each individual feels valued, regardless of their background. This is the vision behind ***diversity and inclusion (D&I) initiatives***. These concepts foster work environments where varied perspectives are not only welcomed but celebrated. In such environments, innovation thrives when diverse teams bring unique viewpoints to the table, leading to creative solutions and better decision-making. When employees feel seen and heard, satisfaction increases, and so does their commitment to the organization, reducing turnover and creating cohesive teams.

The power of diversity lies in its ability to ignite creativity and enhance problem-solving. Diverse teams are like rich tapestries woven with different threads that contribute to the overall strength and beauty of the fabric. When people from different cultural backgrounds and life experiences collaborate, they challenge conventional thinking and introduce fresh ideas.

Diversity of thought is a catalyst for innovation, enabling teams to explore wider arrays of possibilities and approaches. Encouraging varied viewpoints enriches the creative process and equips teams to tackle challenges by drawing effectively from a pool of broad insights and perspectives.

Inclusive environments require intentional effort and commitment to creating spaces where everyone feels respected and valued. Implementing inclusive language and policies is a foundational step in utilizing gender-neutral language, respecting personal pronouns, and ensuring company policies that reflect a commitment to equality and fairness. Moreover, active listening and empathy play crucial roles in building inclusive cultures. Listen genuinely to others and strive to understand their experiences to create a climate of trust and respect. Empathy allows walking in someone else's shoes to foster deeper connections and appreciation for unique perspectives.

Allyship is an active, ongoing process of supporting marginalized groups and advocating equal opportunities. As an ally, you create an inclusive environment by challenging discriminatory behaviors and speaking up when you witness injustice. You might call out biased comments or support initiatives to promote diversity and inclusion. Advocating equal opportunities ensures everyone has access to the same resources and chances for advancement, regardless of background. By actively promoting inclusivity, you contribute to a culture where everyone thrives and diverse voices are heard and amplified.

In the broadest context, embracing diversity and inclusion is a strategic advantage. Companies that prioritize these values often see improved team performance and greater employee engagement (SOURCE 4). Society is increasingly interconnected, and working effectively with people from different backgrounds is more important than ever. Fostering a culture of inclusion enriches your personal and professional life and also contributes to a more just and equitable world.

12

The Pursuit of Continuous Growth and Learning

"Growth is painful. Change is painful. But nothing is as painful as staying stuck somewhere you don't belong."

Mandy Hale

You're standing at the edge of a dense forest, where every path leads to a different adventure. The forest represents the vast opportunities for learning and growth that life offers. Just as each forest trail offers new sights and experiences, lifelong learning opens doors to personal and professional growth you have yet to see. In a world that moves at lightning speed, new technologies and ideas are emerging constantly, and staying relevant means you never stop learning. Lifelong learning keeps your mind flexible and open to change, always ready to adapt to whatever comes next.

12.1 The Importance of Lifelong Learning

In today's ever-evolving job market, continuous learning is essential for keeping up with the latest trends and thriving in an environment where change is always just around the corner. Just as industries transform, so do the skills needed to succeed in them. Lifelong learning makes you a valuable asset in any workplace, equipped and ready to tackle new challenges and roles. Your commitment to learning allows you to explore diverse interests and discover passions you never knew you had. Each new skill adds another skill to your portfolio.

Career advancement often hinges on learning. In a competitive environment, gaining new qualifications and certifications can set you apart by opening doors to new opportunities and responsibilities. Employers value people who are committed to proactive growth and forward-thinking. Moreover, as technology reshapes how you work, your ability to adapt and learn new tools is increasingly important. Staying ahead of technological advancements with up-to-date skills allows you to adapt to change with ease and confidence.

Learning doesn't always require monumental change. Small achievements can make a significant impact. Set aside regular time each week for learning. This is an investment in your future. If you commute, use travel time to learn new trends and concepts by listening to audiobooks or podcasts. This enriches your thinking and makes the journey more enjoyable and productive. Look for opportunities to fit learning into your day whenever possible to facilitate growth as you learn.

There are more diverse learning resources available than ever before.

Online platforms like **Udemy**, **Coursera** and **Mindvalley** offer courses on a wide range of subjects, from personal development to cutting-edge technology that allows learning at your own pace. Those platforms often provide certificates that add to your professional credentials. Community workshops and seminars offer avenues to connect with local experts and peers with common interests that encourage the exchange of ideas and experiences. Informal learning groups provide supportive environments to learn, share insights, and grow together.

12.2 Interactive Element: Personal Learning Plan

- Create a personal learning plan in an area you want to learn more about or a skill you've always wanted to develop.
- Research available resources and set aside time to learn. Your learning plan will keep you focused and motivated as you proceed.
- Keep it flexible and explore unexpected paths you might discover along the way. Be proactive as you learn, grow, and enjoy the world around you and everything it offers.

Example:

Learning Goal	Resources/Materials	Time Commitment	Progress/Notes
Learn Graphic Design	Online course on Canva, YouTube tutorials, design books.	1 hour every evening.	Completed 3 lessons, exploring advanced tools next.
Improve Public Speaking	Join Toastmasters, watch TED Talks, practice presentations with friends.	Weekly club meeting and 2 hours prep.	Practiced a speech, need to work on pacing.

12.3 Developing Critical Thinking Skills

Picture a looming deadline that could impact your immediate future. This is where critical thinking comes into play. At its core, critical thinking is the ability to objectively and rationally evaluate information to examine arguments, identify biases, and assess evidence to reach a conclusion. ***Critical thinking*** is essential to decision-making because it enables you to sift through many factors and focus on choices that are well-informed and rooted in logic. Whether you're choosing a career path, deciding on a major purchase, or sorting through a complex personal dilemma, critical thinking gives you tools to weigh options and choose wisely.

To develop critical thinking skills, read case studies or study real-world situations. When you analyze such events, identify the underlying issues, possible solutions, and visualize potential outcomes.

For example, you've just been assigned a business case study about a failed product launch. Your task would require you to dissect the factors that resulted in failure, from market research errors to ineffective marketing strategies. Examination challenges you to think critically about what went wrong and how it could be rectified.

Similarly, debates and discussions about complex topics sharpen your ability to articulate thoughts clearly and consider different perspectives. Those conversations reinforce your personal views and expose you to alternative viewpoints that broaden your understanding of differing opinions.

Questioning assumptions is another cornerstone of critical thinking. We often operate on ingrained beliefs or societal norms without questioning their validity. Challenging those assumptions encourages the exploration of ideas that lead to understanding and innovation. Think about the biases that fill media reports. Scrutinizing sources and questioning motives help you separate fact from opinion in a world filled with information overload. Challenging conventional wisdom can lead to breakthroughs in thought and practice. Many great innovations stem from questioning the status quo and exploring possibilities that others found impossible.

Critical thinking transcends academic and professional boundaries to find applications in many life issues.

- In business, it enhances negotiation skills to evaluate every position. Your ability to critically assess your opponent's arguments, identify common interests, and propose beneficial solutions can turn a simple negotiation into a successful partnership.
- In personal relationships, critical thinking helps resolve conflicts with win-win approaches. When disagreements arise, evaluate the situation objectively and understand each person's perspective to reduce tension and build a foundation of trust and respect.

Reflection Section

- Think of a recent decision or conflict you faced. Consider how critical thinking might have influenced the outcome.
- Identify biases that affected your perspective and how they might be different in the future.
- Reflection enhances self-awareness and reinforces the value of critical thinking to help you make informed decisions. As you practice these skills, you'll be better equipped to handle your challenges with confidence.

- *Describe the recent decision or conflict.*

....

- *What assumptions did I make in this situation?*

....

- *How did these assumptions shape my approach?*

....

- *Were there any biases that influence my perspective?*

....

- *How could I challenge these biases in the future?*

....

- *How might critical thinking have influenced the outcome?*

....

- *What lessons can I take away to improve future decisions?*

....

12.4 Find Inspiration in Books Instead of Quick Online Fixes

Think of yourself holding a book filled with worlds waiting to be discovered. Books can uniquely delve into deep subjects with a richness that quick online searches often lack. While the internet provides a wealth of information, it also encourages skimming and superficial understanding. You've probably experienced surfing from link to link, gathering snippets of disconnected data. In contrast, books invite you to slow down and explore ideas on a deeper level. They provide in-depth analysis of complex topics for comprehensive exploration and true understanding.

Consider the value of historical context that shapes our perceptions of current events. Books weave narratives that span decades or even centuries with perspectives that illuminate the present to enrich your understanding of real-world experiences. Case studies serve similar functions with detailed examinations of specific instances that illustrate broad principles. Those narratives engage your curiosity and encourage critical thought about how those lessons might apply to your life.

A regular reading habit can transform your approach to learning and personal growth. Set achievable reading goals, like finishing one book a month. This creates a sense of accomplishment and keeps you motivated. A dedicated reading space increases your enjoyment free from distraction. Whether a cozy nook by a window or a comfortable chair in your living room, designate an inviting area to lose yourself in a great book. This space can become a haven where you disconnect from digital noise and immerse yourself in the amazing stories and ideas that books offer.

Books are a wellspring of inspiration, taking you into new realms of thought. ***Thinking Fast and Slow* by Daniel Kahneman** is a treasure trove of insights to explore how we make decisions and the biases that influence them. Kahneman's book challenges you to think about a mindful approach to decision-making.

Meanwhile, ***The Power of Habit* by Charles Duhigg** unravels the science behind habit formation and change, a practical strategy for personal transformation. These books open doors to self-discovery and growth, offering guidance and wisdom you'll remember long after the last page is turned.

The *community aspect of reading* turns solitary activity into shared exploration. Join a local or online book club to connect with others who share your passion for reading, with discussions that deepen your understanding and appreciation of what you read. These groups offer diverse perspectives to enrich your interpretation of the books you read and broaden your horizons. Participate in author events or readings to add another layer of engagement and connect with the creators behind the stories. Those interactions bring books to life, revealing the inspirations that sparked their creation.

Reading as a regular part of your life cultivates a habit that feeds your mind and soul. Books offer more than information; they are pathways to wisdom, reflection, and growth. As you explore different genres and topics, you expand your worldview and gain insights that influence actions and choices. Your commitment to reading can foster a lifelong love of learning, **nurturing curiosity and creativity.**

In a world that prioritizes speed and convenience, books remind you about the value of depth and contemplation. They invite us to slow down, savor the beauty of language and the power of ideas. Choosing books over quick online fixes shows you a ***rich, meaningful view of the world*** around you. On your journey of continuous growth and learning, let books be your guide to inspiration and wisdom along the way.

As you close this chapter, remember that books are more than just words on a page—they are gateways to ***new perspectives and possibilities***. Embrace the stories and insights they offer to enrich your life and fuel your growth. Remember that the knowledge and inspiration you've gained from reading empower you to face new challenges confidently with creativity throughout life.

Conclusion

You have successfully reached the end of your journey through *Modern Life Skills for Young Adults 2.0*. Take a moment to reflect on the path we've traveled together. You have explored a multitude of skills to navigate the complexities of modern life today. From conquering procrastination to mastering time management, each chapter has hopefully equipped you with practical tools to empower living and enjoy life on your terms.

The heart of this book is my vision to help you achieve and enjoy independence without overwhelm. My goal has been to provide you with insights to make adulting less daunting and more adventurous. Along the way, you've delved into the art of managing finances, building meaningful relationships, and cultivating an entrepreneurial mindset. These are not just life skills; you have built a ***solid foundation for a balanced life.***

The key takeaways from our joint exploration include overcoming procrastination by understanding its roots and applying strategies like the Pomodoro technique. We've also highlighted the essence of financial literacy: budgeting, savings, and investing. Those fundamentals position you for lifelong success. Strong, valuable relationships add depth to life by embracing an entrepreneurial mindset that encourages innovation and resilience.

As you move forward, remember that life is a ***continuous journey of growth.*** Mistakes are opportunities (not failures) to learn and develop. Embrace a growth mindset that welcomes challenges as stepping stones. Each step you take, whether forward or back, contributes to your personal development.

I encourage you to seize and apply the knowledge you've acquired within these pages. Actively practice the exercises, test the strategies, and reflect on your personal experiences to chart your progress. Weave the skills you've learned into your daily routine and future aspirations. This book is a tool; true power lies in your willingness to use it.

Reflection is a powerful tool for growth. Challenge yourself to implement what you've learned into your daily life. *What changes can you make today to achieve a more fulfilled and independent existence?* Take time to think deeply about your goals and the steps needed to achieve them.

Learning is a journey that never ends. Continually seek new resources—books, courses, or conversations with mentors. Commit to lifelong learning and personal development because the world is ever-evolving. Cultivate curiosity and seek new knowledge to maintain adaptability and resilience.

As this book concludes, know that you have the tools to create a successful, meaningful life. You possess the strength to navigate challenges and the wisdom to seize opportunities. Exercise confidence in your ability to shape your future. Remember, the journey is yours to make; it is rich with potential and promise.

Thank you for allowing me to share this space with you on your journey; it has been my great honor. I hope this book is a guiding light inspiring you to embrace the rich possibilities that lie ahead. Your story is just beginning; it is destined to be remarkable.

Wishing you every success!

DBJ

> **"Hard skills might get your foot in the door. It is soft skills that keep you thriving."**
>
> *Daily Balance Journals*

Your Thoughts Matter!

Congratulations on learning the essentials of managing procrastination, making money, fostering strong relationships, and enjoying independence without overwhelm! Your journey doesn't end here; it can be a beacon for others just starting their own.

By sharing your thoughts on Amazon, you *guide fellow young adults* to this valuable resource and continue the cycle of learning and improvement. Your review can light the way for someone else seeking to balance their ambitions with their personal life, just as you have.

Scan the QR code to leave your review on Amazon. Each word you write helps deepen our community's knowledge and reach.

Thank you for your invaluable support! Together, we're not just reading a book—we're passing on a legacy of empowerment and growth. Your participation is sincerely appreciated.

References

Why People Procrastinate: The Psychology and Causes of ... https://solvingprocrastination.com/why-people-procrastinate/

Pomodoro Technique: History, Steps, Benefits, and ... https://www.verywellmind.com/pomodoro-technique-history-steps-benefits-and-drawbacks-6892111

17 Top Productivity Apps For Students (2023): Best GPA ... https://medium.com/@hopesource318/17-top-productivity-apps-for-students-2023-best-gpa-ever-f47503b2ae5

Embracing Imperfection and Growth as a Leader https://www.linkedin.com/pulse/overcoming-perfectionism-embracing-imperfection-growth-leader-gjuae

The Eisenhower Matrix: How to prioritize your to-do list https://asana.com/resources/eisenhower-matrix

Time Blocking — Your Complete Guide to More Focused ... https://todoist.com/productivity-methods/time-blocking

The Power of Digital Detox: Unlocking Productivity ... https://medium.com/@florian.schroeder.bln/the-power-of-digital-detox-unlocking-productivity-through-switching-off-ca20b96cdc4b

Module 6: How to Say "No" Assertively https://www.cci.health.wa.gov.au/~/media/CCI/Consumer-Modules/Assert-Yourself/Assert-Yourself---06---How-to-Say-No-Assertively.pdf

Decision-Making Frameworks for Youth | Restackio https://www.restack.io/p/technology-for-youth-participation-answer-decision-making-frameworks

Don't Just Tell Students to Solve Problems. Teach Them How. https://today.ucsd.edu/story/dont-just-tell-students-to-solve-problems-teach-them-to

7 Strategies to Make Decisions with Clarity and Confidence https://www.psychologytoday.com/us/blog/the-path-to-passionate-happiness/202109/7-strategies-to-make-decisions-with-clarity-and

11 Famous Failures That Will Inspire You to Success https://www.inc.com/scott-mautz/11-famous-failures-that-will-inspire-you-to-succes.html

The importance of self-care for maintaining mental health https://today.marquette.edu/2024/08/the-importance-of-self-care-for-maintaining-mental-health/

Strategies for Eating Well on a Budget - The Nutrition Source https://nutritionsource.hsph.harvard.edu/strategies-nutrition-budget/

8 Quick and Effective Workouts for Busy Professionals https://fitnessproject.us/blog/8-quick-and-effective-workouts-for-busy-professionals/

Mental Health and Sleep https://www.sleepfoundation.org/mental-health

Mindfulness in University Students: A Tool for Managing ... https://scholarsarchive.byu.edu/cgi/viewcontent.cgi?article=1094&context=familyperspectives

Resilience: Build skills to endure hardship https://www.mayoclinic.org/tests-procedures/resilience-training/in-depth/resilience/art-20046311

Caring for Your Mental Health https://www.nimh.nih.gov/health/topics/caring-for-your-mental-health

Signs of needing help for mental health, drugs, alcohol https://www.samhsa.gov/find-support/how-to-cope/signs-of-needing-help

Active listening tips, skills, techniques, and examples https://www.mindtools.com/az4wxv7/active-listening

Youth Conflict Resolution Techniques + Life Skills https://elcentronc.org/advocacy/youth-conflict-resolution-techniques-life-skills-processing-conflict-during-a-crisis/

Trust, Safety, and Respect - The Importance of Boundaries https://studentaffairs.stanford.edu/how-life-treeting-you-importance-of-boundaries#:~

Dating and Relationships in the Digital Age https://www.pewresearch.org/internet/2020/05/08/dating-and-relationships-in-the-digital-age/

Ultimate Guide to Off-Campus Student Housing - Outpost Club https://outpost-club.com/blog/ultimate-guide-to-off-campus-student-housing

Studying 101: Study Smarter Not Harder - UNC Learning Center https://learningcenter.unc.edu/tips-and-tools/studying-101-study-smarter-not-harder/

How to Balance Work & School: 7 Strategies - HBS Online https://online.hbs.edu/blog/post/how-to-balance-work-and-school

10 Benefits of Extracurricular Activities in College https://www.psychologytoday.com/us/blog/social-lights/202309/10-benefits-of-extracurricular-activities-in-college

Effective networking strategies for career growth https://careers.intuitive.com/en/employee-stories/career-growth-advice/effective-networking-strategies-for-career-growth/

How to Write a Cover Letter [2024 Guide, Tips, & Examples] https://www.tealhq.com/post/how-to-write-a-cover-letter-the-ultimate-guide#:~

15 Expert Job Interview Tips To Get Hired Faster In 2024 https://www.forbes.com/sites/bryanrobinson/2024/04/05/15-expert-job-interview-tips-to-get-hired-faster-in-2024/

Tips for Adjusting to New Workplace Cultures and Customs - 6Q https://6q.io/blog/new-workplace-cultures-and-customs/

10 Essential Money Tips For Young Adults https://www.forbes.com/sites/enochomololu/2023/09/18/10-essential-money-tips-for-young-adults/

References

Your guide to creating a budget plan - Better Money Habits https://bettermoneyhabits.bankofamerica.com/en/saving-budgeting/creating-a-budget

Using Credit Scores to Understand Predictors and ... https://pmc.ncbi.nlm.nih.gov/articles/PMC6187788/#:~

How to file your federal income tax return https://www.usa.gov/file-taxes

Entrepreneurial Mindset - 10 Most Crucial Characteristics ... https://www.nexford.edu/insights/entrepreneurial-mindset

Intrapreneurship Examples To Learn From https://lmarks.com/blog/intrapreneurship-examples-to-learn-from/

Resilience: The Unsung Skill of Successful Entrepreneurs https://doodle.com/en/resilience-the-unsung-skill-of-successful-entrepreneurs/

11 Reasons Why Networking is Essential for Any Startup https://www.universitylabpartners.org/blog/networking-essential-for-startup

Remote Work Productivity: Strategies and Tips for Success ... https://www.officernd.com/blog/remote-work-productivity/

The Ultimate Guide to Building a Personal Brand https://careers.intuitive.com/en/employee-stories/career-growth-advice/the-ultimate-guide-to-building-a-personal-brand/

Mastering Digital Etiquette: Essential Tips for 2023 - Gistly https://gist.ly/youtube-summarizer/mastering-digital-etiquette-essential-tips-for-2023

Why Is Diversity and Inclusion in the Workplace Important? https://www.greatplacetowork.com/resources/blog/why-is-diversity-inclusion-in-the-workplace-important

8 reasons why continuous learning is crucial for career ... https://www.cornerstoneondemand.com/resources/article/8-reasons-why-continuous-learning-is-crucial-for-career-growth/

Be a Better Thinker With These 7 Critical Thinking Exercises https://able.ac/blog/critical-thinking-exercises/

Reading on-screen vs reading in print https://natlib.govt.nz/blog/posts/reading-on-screen-vs-reading-in-print-whats-the-difference-for-learning

The 25 Top Self-Help Books For Personal Growth - Forbes https://www.forbes.com/sites/entertainment/article/best-self-help-books/

Printed in Great Britain
by Amazon